TO BE A C
An Introduction to Christian Believing, Living, and Prayer

JOHN BARNES

The Canterbury Press
Norwich

© John Barnes 1994

First published 1994 by The Canterbury Press Norwich
(a publishing imprint of Hymns Ancient & Modern Limited,
a registered charity)
St Mary's Works, St Mary's Plain,
Norwich, Norfolk, NR3 3BH

British Library Cataloguing in Publication Data

A catalogue record for this book is available
from the British Library

ISBN 1–85311–084–1

*Typeset by Datix International Limited
Bungay, Suffolk and
Printed and bound in Great Britain by
St Edmundsbury Press Limited
Bury St Edmunds, Suffolk*

CONTENTS

PREFACE

Working as an Anglican priest I have long felt the need of a small book which gives a fairly orderly and reasonably simple account of the Christian religion. The kind of book which could be used by an adult preparing for confirmation, by someone wanting a kind of 'refresher course', perhaps during Lent, or indeed by anyone who may be seeking information about Christian belief and practice.

In attempting to write such a book I have allowed the three elements in religion to dictate its form. First, the credal element – what is believed – and this is fundamental not least because action is ultimately based upon belief. Second, the moral element – how a person lives, and the kind of character which he or she is seeking to develop. Third, the whole area of prayer and worship – spirituality – which covers the personal relationship which the individual enjoys with God and to some extent with his or her fellow believers. The word 'prayer', used here to describe the third element in religion, is clearly being used with a wide reference.

So this book has three parts, each dealing with one of the elements in religion, and each part is divided into ten short sections. The part concerning belief is based upon the Apostles' Creed, the part concerning behaviour upon the Ten Commandments, and the part concerning spirituality is based upon the Lord's Prayer. It seemed good to have these primary texts as foundations for the three sections of the book, even though doing so has imposed certain contraints as regards both the material offered and the order of its presentation.

Maybe it is foolhardy to attempt to deal with a vast subject in a small book such as this, and certainly there are inevitably omissions and limitations. I am only too aware of these, and must remind the reader that this book claims only to be an introduction to Christian belief, living, and prayer. One obvious limitation is the fact that nothing is said about the history of the Church, whereas the history of any body of thought, or body of people, is vital to understanding both it and them. Perhaps this is especially so in the case of the Church, in view of the fact that God, the Christian believes, continues to manifest himself in the life of the Church, and this in a dynamic way. Jesus promised that the Holy Spirit would lead his followers into all truth (John 14:26), and it is important to discern and appreciate this. Again, nothing is said of the divisions within christendom, despite the fact that one of the most apparent characteristics of the Church is the fact that it is not, at least in the most obvious sense, One.

Bearing in mind the fact of division within the universal Church, it might be asked what, or rather whose, are the teachings to be found here? Is it an Anglican view of the Christian faith which is being presented? And if so, from which school of thought within the Anglican tradition does it come? My hope is that I have set down what might be called 'main stream' Christian teaching: the essential teaching which has been accepted by the major part of christendom all down the centuries, and which a large number of people who have a reverence of Holy Scripture and of the age-old tradition of the Church, will find accords more or less with what they have both received and sought to live by.

There is one further limitation which ought to be mentioned, and this is the fact that I have not attempted any kind of Christian apologetic. My aim has been to give a simple statement of what Christians believe and practise, and it has not seemed appropriate to attempt to produce arguments concerning why they think and act as they do. I would hope, however, that the inner coherence, reasonableness, and indeed attractiveness, of the Christian religion as it has been tradition-ally understood, will be apparent to the reader.

Finally, I wish to express my thanks to Mary Johnson for her kindness in typing the manuscript.

Wymondham, Norfolk   JOHN BARNES
Michaelmas 1993

PART ONE
Christian Belief

CHRISTIAN BELIEF

1

'We believe in one God, the Father, the Almighty . . .'

What lies at the heart of Religion? It is the belief, the awareness, that over and above the visible word there is some kind of Being which controls our destiny. A Being which is powerful, and in whose presence we feel awe. A Being which demands our worship and our obedience, and which can only be described by such absolutes as 'Almighty' and 'Eternal'. We call this Being God.

In the Christian Religion we assert that this God has caused us to exist, together with all creation. But we also believe that we human beings are different from the rest of creation in so far as we have been made 'in God's image'. This means that however weak and fallible we may be, we nevertheless mirror, reflect, our Maker. We do this chiefly in so far as we are rational beings, capable of thought; creative beings, capable of designing, inventing, planning; and loving beings, capable of relationships which are founded upon more than mere self-interest. Since we are made in God's image, reflecting his likeness in our rationality, creativeness and ability to love, we believe further that we can learn about God our Maker by studying man at his highest and best. And further we believe that we can discover an insight into our meaning and purpose by reflecting upon why it is that a man and a woman themselves with to procreate, wish to have children. They want children so that those children might both receive and return their love. In rather the same way we believe that God made man so that man might both be the object of God's boundless love, and might also return that love. We are made, in other words, to love God and to be loved by him. This, we believe, is both the reason for our creation and the purpose of our life: to love God, and to receive his love for us.

Now if we are to love God it is necessary that we should know him. And if that is to happen, then God must reveal himself, show himself, to us. He must take the initiative, for there is comparatively little that our minds can work out about God unaided. Knowledge must come from him. But how can man, with his very limited understanding, begin to take-in such knowledge? How can we begin to assimilate so great and wonderful a mystery as the Being and Nature of God? How could – and how did – God begin to teach mankind about himself?

We believe that he began this long and gradual process by choosing a special people, the people which became the Jewish nation. A people whom he enabled over many centuries to grasp certain truths about himself. Amongst those truths, two were of special importance. First, the truth that God is One. One rather than many – a very different view from that held by other nations in the ancient world, who believed in many gods and goddesses, each with their own concerns and territories. The second truth which God brought his people to see is this: that he is a God who loves and cares for his people in such a way that it is appropriate to call him 'Father'. He is not a God who is hostile or indifferent, but one who looks upon his people with love and compassion.

'Father': a picture, an image, taken from human life, from our own experience, and applied to God. And there are other images too which God used in the process of revealing himself, in showing his Nature. 'King' and 'Shepherd', for example. In effect, God said to his people 'I am like a Father', 'I am like a King', 'I am like a Shepherd'. You know what those things are; this is how you should think of me. And so he enabled them to think and speak about the One who is in truth beyond and above all thought and all speech, too great and too wonderful for us to know by the normal ways by which we come to know and understand things.

So far we have touched upon some of those important words which come at the very beginning of the Christian

Creed: 'Father', 'God', 'Almighty', 'One'. But nothing has been said about the first word 'Believe'. 'I believe'. Note that we do not begin the Creed by saying 'I know'. Nor, on the other hand, by saying 'I imagine'. We say 'I believe'. Which means 'I accept', 'I accept as true'. We admit that we cannot have absolute certainty about anything in this life. We do not pretend to have what we have not, and indeed cannot have. 'I believe' means 'I have weighed things up, and I maintain that there are very good grounds for saying . . .' Such good grounds that I am prepared to live and act and think upon the presumption that these things are true.

2

'Maker of heaven and earth, of all that is, seen and unseen . . .'

Why did God make us? – so that we might both receive and return his love. Now if we are to love him, we must first know him, and for this reason he wishes to reveal himself to mankind. He began the process of revelation by choosing the Jewish people, whom he gradually brought to understand that he is One God, present and powerful everywhere – Almighty – and that furthermore he is a God who loves and cares for mankind: a Father, a Shepherd, to his people. From here, it would be logical to think of how the gradual process of revelation all led up to that point in time when God revealed himself in the fulness of truth by the coming amongst us, God the Son, Jesus, the Word made Flesh. But before we reach that point, the words of the Creed bid us to think of God as Creator, 'Maker of Heaven and earth'. And certainly in his work of creation God does in another way reveal himself to us, just as a fine craftsman reveals something of himself in the things which he designs and makes. So it is fitting that before we go on to think about God revealing himself in Christ, we should pause to consider how he shows himself to us in the created order.

'Maker of heaven and earth'. Too often we take those words in the sense of 'The One who made' rather than in the sense of 'The One who made and who is making'. For it is easy for us to see Creation just as something which happened a very long time ago, a work which is now finished and complete. I suppose the story of the Six-Day Creation in Genesis encourages us to think like that – the ancient story which does not pretend to be a piece of scientific history but is rather a parable, a story with a meaning. As a parable, it is successful: it makes the point that everything that exists has its origin in God the Creator in a vivid way. But in making God sound like

8

a divine conjuror who pulls a different white rabbit out of the hat for six days running, it scarcely gives expression to the wonder, complexity and indeed time-scale of Creation. It does, too, suggest that God finished his creative work a long time ago, and then left his world and his universe to its own devices.

But the truth is different. God's work as Creator, and indeed as Sustainer of the created order, has never ceased. Our present existence shows this. His creative work is going on now, and we are part of it. Vegetation springs up, and all forms of life continue to develop. People are conceived and born, new people who did not exist before, and the whole face of the earth is changing as the centuries and millenia pass by. The Creator is at work, and we are surrounded and upheld not just by the results of his works done long ago, but by the creative activity itself. 'Maker': not just the One who has made once, long ago, but the One who is making now, and whose creative power has never ceased. It is all infinitely more wonderful than we sometimes suppose.

In what he makes, in his creativity and its expression, God does indeed give us insight into his nature. We see the glory of his immense power in the vastness of space. We see his majesty and beauty reflected in the objects which he as brought into being. We see his care and his wisdom in the intricacy and inter-relation of all that is. We see his love in providing so richly for the delight and sustenance of mankind. 'The heavens proclaim the glory of God, and the firmament shows forth his handiwork', the psalmist wrote (Psalm 19:1).

But of course what we now see and know and understand is only a part of what God has made and is making. 'Maker of heaven and earth, and of all that is, seen and unseen'. We know little as yet of the nature of heaven, and so we have to think of that state of blessedness and perfect joy in earthly terms – in terms of field and banquets, crowns and mansions. We know little, too, of the being of the Holy Angels, that part of creation which is wholly spiritual, as against rocks and rivers which are purely material, and man who is a combination of the material and the spiritual. We know little, for that matter, about our own soul, that mysterious and indefinable part of us which is additional to our physical and mental being, and which is that part of us which enables us to relate to God. Nor do we know all that is to be known about the material world, as is shown by the fact that discoveries about all kinds of things continue to be made day by day. As yet we know and understand only a fraction of what God the Creator has made. So much remains to be revealed to us: so much which will give us new insight into the wonder and glory and power of God who is 'Maker of heaven and earth, of all things seen and unseen'.

Let us remember two things, though. First, that all which is made by God is good. Good in essence, because he is its source. Capable of pollution by man, yet always good in its essential nature. The material world no less than the spiritual is there to be enjoyed, appreciated – there for us to take delight in. And capable, too, of showing God to us. Second, let us also remember that what is made by God and reveals him to us, is to be treated with reverence. To waste, exploit, damage, or wantonly destroy any part of creation is, for the Christian, a kind of blasphemy. Man has been set over the material part of creation to be a wise and just steward. To cherish as well as to enjoy it, even as he cherishes the immortal soul which God has given to him. The seen and the unseen both come from God and belong to God. We are to enjoy but also reverence what he has chosen to share with us.

3

'We believe in one Lord, Jesus Christ, the only Son of God . . .'

Mankind, created by God, has two fundamental needs. The first is to know God (in so far as that is possible, given the limitations of man's understanding) – to know both God's nature and his will for man. Then, second, mankind needs reconciliation with God, so that the rift which has come about through our disobedience may be healed, and we may be restored to that endless life and delight which God intended us to enjoy from the beginning. In our Lord Jesus Christ both of these needs – our need to know God, and our need to be reconciled to God – are met. Jesus 'shows us the Father', and he reunites us with the Father.

Who is this Jesus Christ of whom we read in the Gospels, and who is so central to the Christian Faith that both it and we bear his title in being called 'Christians'? He is (and the Creed almost labours the point, it having been worked out in the face of bitter controversy) God. God the Son. Not in any sense less than the Father, or inferior to him, but of 'one being' with the Father, sharing in his essential nature, 'true God from true God'. 'Not made', not, that is, a creature, but 'eternally begotten'. Of these various phrases, it is probably the one which proclaims him to be 'of one being with the Father' which speaks most clearly and insistently. Truly God, from eternity, and yet also from a certain point in time – that point in time at which he became miraculously present in the womb of a human Mother so as to take flesh – also man, and truly man. God incarnate, God 'enfleshed', and yet without in any sense ceasing to be divine. Furthermore, in Christ the human and the divine were in no mere loose association: we express this by speaking of his 'One Person', but within that one person there were two Natures, the divine nature, his from eternity, and

11

also the human nature, existing from that moment when Mary said to the angel 'let it be to me according to your word' (Luke 1:38), whereupon the second person of the Holy Trinity entered (without human intercourse, which would have been both unnecessary and inappropriate) into the Virgin's womb to share in our human nature.

Now this Incarnation of God the Son – his taking of a human body, mind, and soul – happened so that the two fundamental needs of mankind could be met. The first of those needs, we recall, is that we might know God, and we can think of God the Son coming amongst us at his incarnation in terms of God 'coming down to our level' so that we might be able to know him. In, perhaps, rather the way that someone wishing to teach young children, whose experience is necessarily limited, has to 'come down to their level'. Such a teacher will not present young children with abstract ideas. Maybe he or she will show them pictures. There is a sense in which Jesus is a picture, or Icon, of God. God with us so that he can be seen and heard and touched. God come amongst us, Immanuel, God-with-us. So that in the things which Jesus said, and which are recorded in the Gospels, we can hear in human words, and so understand, the divine wisdom. And in the things which he did and which are recorded there we can see, see and understand, the divine power and the divine love. We have thought already of how God shows us something of himself in the natural world which he has brought into being, and also of how he taught the Jewish people in the course of many centuries that he is One God, present everywhere, all-powerful, and a God who loves and cares for his people. But in Jesus, God come amongst us, God 'come down to our level', God's showing of himself to us reaches a glorious climax. The light does indeed shine in the darkness. Here truly is divine self-disclosure. So that when Philip says to Jesus 'Show us the Father and we shall be satisfied', Jesus makes the profound reply 'He who has seen me has seen the Father' (John 14: 8–9).

In the next section we must think of how Jesus meets that

second fundamental need of man, the need for reconciliation with God. But before that, an observation. Jesus began his two-fold work of revelation and redemption by becoming man, by taking our flesh. Already man had the dignity of being created in the divine image, of sharing in the rationality, creativeness, and capacity for unselfish love which belong to God. Now, by the incarnation, our humanity is further dignified and enhanced by Jesus, God the Son, sharing in that humanity. As the poet John Donne wrote:

> *'Twas much, that man was made like God before,*
> *But, that God should be made like man, much more* *

But this double honour, of being made in God's image, and of God the Son having shared in our human nature, belongs to all people. It is shared by the poor, the disabled, the underprivileged and the unbelieving. By those we find it easy to despise and set at naught, by those to whom we think ourselves superior, by those we scorn and deride. The Christian knows that he must be very careful that he does not scorn, deride, despise or neglect Christ, who shares in this common humanity. For Jesus has taught us to seek him, and serve him, in everyone whom he has made and who, by his incarnation, have become his brothers and sisters.

* John Donne, *Holy Sonnets* XV

4

'For us men and for our salvation he came down from heaven . . .'

By becoming man, Jesus met that first great need of ours: the need to know about God. For by his becoming man, we were able to experience God in human terms. Rather as if a piece of writing had been translated into a language which we understand. Equally, Jesus as God made Man met that second need: our need to be reconciled with God.

We must begin by examining this second need. It stems from the fact that God, in creating man in his own image, gave man that ability to think and choose which we call free-will. We are not robots, incapable of making real choices: no loving parent would want his or her child to be like that. We can choose the good, indeed we can choose God. But the corollary of this is that we can also choose the bad. Man, through possessing free-will, can choose to disobey God; he can choose to destroy rather than build, to hate rather than love, to grasp rather than give. He can choose not to obey those wise directives which God has given him for his well-being; he can ignore the law of God which was summed up so briefly but so completely in Our Lord's two commandments 'Love God, and love your neighbour'. Man, having the dignity of free-will, can choose the way of disobedience, and he has consistently done so. We call this disobedience sin: an ugly word for an ugly thing. Now this disobedience in which all of us share has cut us off from God. We are in rebellion against him. We are in truth 'no more worthy to be called his sons'. Such is the perfection of God's holiness that man's disobedience made an impassable rift between him and his creature. A rift which caused mankind to lose all claim to the endless life and fulness of joy which God had intended for us. Through disobedience by sin, man came to deserve not eternal life, but eternal

punishment: the punishment of an endless and complete separation from God, who is the source of all joy and delight.

But however fickle man might be, God's love for him is
firm and unchanging. So that God wished to restore man to his
inheritance, and bring to an end that separation which sin had
brought about. In order to do this, God chose to become Man.
To board, as it were, the sinking ship of humanity so that he
might rescue it. But how, we might ask, could this be done:
what were the mechanics of Our Lord's work of redemption?
In so far as we can penetrate the profound mystery of our
Salvation, it worked like this. Jesus, God the Son, took flesh of
a human Mother. Flesh, humanity, that was unstained by sin,
and so not alienated from God. By becoming man, he could be
our Representative and act on our behalf, something which he
could not have done without sharing in our common manhood.
Then, as our Representative, he could do the two things by
which our redemption was brought about.

First, he could bear on our behalf and in our place, a
token of the punishment due to man on account of his disobedience: punishment which the perfect Justice of God demands
should be exacted, but which the perfect love of God makes
him wish to bear himself, in our place. We believe that this is
what was happening in the course of Our Lord's suffering,
which culminated in his cruel death upon the Cross. We
believe that in the course of his passion he was 'paying the
price of sin', so that the way might thereafter be open for us to
receive God's forgiveness whenever we admit our faults, and
ask for that forgiveness. The punishment which justice requires
to precede restoration has been dealt with. Then second, by
taking our manhood and thereby being able to represent us,
we believe that Jesus was able to offer himself to the Father on
our behalf. Offer his perfect humanity which, being
untarnished by sin, was acceptable to the Father. We would
see Jesus as offering himself to the Father throughout his
incarnate life, but we would also see this self-offering as
reaching a climax upon the Cross. Indeed we sometimes speak

of the 'altar' of the Cross, an altar being a place where an offering, a sacrifice, is made to God.

But how does this fact that Jesus has offered himself to the Father on our behalf, and that his offering has been accepted, affect us individually? It does so because the effects of what Jesus has done are applied to us, and more particularly they are applied to us in the Sacraments of Holy Baptism and Holy Communion. In these Sacraments, under the outward signs of water and bread and wine, Jesus shares with us the new life which which he has risen from the dead. This Easter life, which is the life of Christ, flows into us at the Font, and it is built up in us as we receive the Body and Blood of Christ at the Altar. By these gifts we are joined to Christ, united with him. We become branches of that true vine which is Christ. Now if we are made one with the Christ who has offered himself to the Father, and who, as the writer of the Letter to the Hebrews teaches us, continues to make his perfect and acceptable self-offering in heaven (Hebrews 9: 23–24), then it follows that we too are accepted by God. Accepted in Christ, as his members, and thereby reconciled with the Father. So the mechanics of salvation have two aspects: Christ has suffered in our humanity and in our place, thereby opening the way to forgiveness. He has also offered himself to the Father, and we who are sharers in his risen life are offered and accepted as part of that offering.

In this glorious plan, 'the scheme of our redemption', which Our Lord has carried through out of his great love for us, the Eucharist has a vital place: the Eucharist, the rite in which we commemorate and make present our Lord's dying and rising for us, and which lies at the heart of the life and worship of the Church. For in the Eucharist we do two things which are integral to our redemption. We place before God, and we plead, that offering or sacrifice which Jesus has made and which he continues to make in heaven. We say in effect the words found in a popular eucharistic hymn:

Look, Father, look on his anointed face,
*and only look on us as found in him.**

We also receive Jesus in Holy Communion, so that our life continues to be bound up with his, and we thereby remain acceptable and accepted as part of his self-offering. Whenever the Christian comes to the altar, his redemption is being worked out and brought nearer to fruition. Our Lord continues his saving work, answering that second basic need which we have, the need for reconciliation with God, from whom we have become estranged by sin.

* *New English Hymnal* 273

5

'We believe in the Holy Spirit, the Lord, the giver of life . . .'

Lurking in the minds of many people, I believe, are two mistaken ideas about God the Holy Spirit. The first is that when he came to the apostles on the Day of Pentecost under the signs of fire and wind, he was then making his first appearance upon the stage of Creation. The second mistaken idea is that the coming at Pentecost was also the last appearance of the Holy Spirit. Both ideas are very mistaken indeed.

In the Christian Religion we assert that the Holy Spirit is divine; we speak of God the Holy Spirit, and we say in the Creed that he 'proceeds from the Father and the Son' and that 'with the Father and the Son he is worshipped and glorified'. If he is God, then it follows that he has existed from eternity, and also that his existence can have no ending. This is something fundamental about God, a fact about his nature. It is one of the things that makes God essentially different from us his creatures. It is, too, something which we find it difficult to grasp. Everything other than God has a limited extension in time – a beginning and an end. God alone is eternal, outside time. Which is one reason why the question which children sometimes ask 'Who made God' really has no meaning.

But the Christian Faith says more about the Holy Spirit than that he has existed from eternity. We believe that he has been intimately involved in the continuing work of Creation, Revelation and Redemption from the beginning. It is good that amongst those few statements which we make about the Holy Spirit in the Creed is the one 'he has spoken through the prophets', because that takes us into the Old Testament straight away. But we need to go further back than the prophets. Back, in fact, to the very first sentence of the Bible, where we read that the Spirit 'hovered over the abyss' at the beginning of

Creation. We speak properly of the 'Creator Spirit', one with the Father and the Son 'through whom all things were made' (John 1:3) in bringing into being all that is. The Creator Spirit, and, as God reveals himself in the life and history of his chosen people, the Enabling Spirit, too. For in the Old Testament we see the Holy Spirit being given to specific people to enable them to carry out specific tasks. To Bezalel and Aholiab, for example, enabling them to instruct the artists and craftsmen who made the Tabernacle in the desert (Exodus 31:1–6); to Joshua, enabling him to assist and to succeed Moses (Numbers 27:15–18); to Jephthah, enabling him to conquer the Ammonites (Judges 11:29). But the prophet Joel foretold that a time would come when the Spirit would be given to all God's people, and not just to those entrusted with special tasks and functions (Joel 2:28–29). This prophecy, we believe, was fulfilled at Pentecost, when the Holy Spirit was poured out upon the apostles, and then upon all believers (Acts 2:1–4).

Upon all believers, and in every age. Because just as all Christians share in the apostolic task of witnessing to Our Lord Jesus Christ, so they also share in that enabling Gift given to the apostles at Pentecost – the Holy Spirit who came to the apostles under the signs of fire and wind. At baptism, the Spirit comes to each person, the same Spirit, but under a different sign: not fire and wind, but water poured out. Like the baptismal waters, the Holy Spirit is poured out upon all who receive this Sacrament, as Joel foretold. So that the Christian becomes, in that memorable phrase of St Paul, a 'temple'Jof the Holy Spirit. He comes to the Christian because he is, as we state in the Creed, 'the Lord, the giver of life'. He comes to communicate that resurrection life of Jesus, just as he came so wonderfully and mysteriously to Mary to be the means whereby she conceived the Divine Word in her womb. Indeed he comes to the Christian to form Christ within him or her. To make us little by little and just as far as we will allow him, Christ-like. The Creator Spirit, the Enabling Spirit, comes to us to conform us, and to enable us to be conformed, to the pattern of our Lord's perfect humanity. He does this by those other gifts, over and above the gift of life itself, which he brings to us. St Paul listed them: love, joy, peace, patience, kindness, goodness, fidelity, gentleness, self-control (Galatians 5:22). He calls them 'fruits of the Spirit': they are fruits which can be produced within the life of the Christian – in obedience to our Lord's commands that his disciples should bear fruit – if, by the Spirit, the Christian is grafted into that True Vine which is Christ. The Creator Spirit, the Enabling Spirit, and also the Sanctifying Spirit. The One who makes the Christian disciple holy as he comes to grow in the likenes of Christ.

Perhaps it is more difficult for the Christian to think and speak about God the Holy Spirit than it is for him to think and speak about God the Father and God the Son. Which may be why God himself has provided those powerful images of fire and wind; images which evoke within us some sense of the being and nature of the Holy Spirit (Acts 2:2–3). Fire, which speaks of warmth, the warm of that love which is the principal gift of the Spirit, and of heat which both melts and consumes. Fire, which like the unseen wind is never still, always active, and so difficult to contain and describe. But there is a third image of the Spirit, which no less than fire and wind has been given to us: the image of the dove, the sign under which the Spirit descended upon Jesus at his baptism in Jordan (Mark 1:10). This is an image which both surprises and perplexes, for it seems to speak of weakness rather than strength. The seeming scandal of this third image of the Spirit, an image which seems to be incapable of expressing the power and wonder of God the Holy Spirit, speaks plainly however of the scandal of the divine gentleness, courtesy and vulnerability. Of the incredible, scandalous fact that God the Holy Spirit condescends to come quietly and unseen into the heedless, unresponsive hearts of Christian people, there to mould and to melt, to guide and to renew, but only as far and as quickly as the individual permits.

6

'We believe in the Holy Spirit . . . who proceeds from the Father and the Son. With the Father and the Son he is worshipped and glorified . . .'

Having thought about each of the Persons of the Holy Trinity individually, God the Father, God the Son, and God the Holy Spirit, we must think again about the oneness, the unit, of God. We believe that God chose the Jewish people long ago, and gradually brought them to an understanding of what he is like, a process which is recorded in the Old Testament. One of the most basic facts which was revealed in this way was the truth that there is one God, and not a whole college of gods. For Christianity as for Judaism, belief in one God is fundamental. Yet we believe that within that essential unity or oneness God has, in the fulness of time, revealed himself as Trinity. We assert that within the Godhead there is a Trinity of Persons, Father, Son, and Holy Spirit, and that the three persons are 'of the same substance' and 'equal in majesty'. This belief in the Holy Trinity lies at the heart of the Christian religion, and at the heart of Christian spirituality.

Now we believe that God has shown himself to man as Trinity in terms of divine activity. In other words we know God's nature through what he has done and is doing. Three questions are asked before baptism: 'Do you belive and trust in God the Father, who made the world? Do you believe and trust in his Son Jesus Christ, who redeemed the world? Do you believe and trust in the Holy Spirit, who gives life to the people of God?' Making, redeeming, enlivening: we know God by what he does, for this is how he has chosen to reveal himself to us. Yet whilst we particularly associate creation with the Father, redemption with the Son, and enlivening or sanctify-

21

ing with the Spirit, we must never think of the three Persons of the Holy Trinity working independently or in isolation. None of the Persons ever 'goes it alone'. God is three: but he is also eternally and essentially One. So that each of the three Persons is intimately associated in whatever activity we assign in our thinking to any one particular Person. For example, we speak of the Father as 'Maker of heaven and earth' at the beginning of the Creed. Yet later in the same Creed we say of Jesus, God the Son, 'through whom all things were made'. We also speak of the 'Creator Spirit', having been led to do so by his 'brooding on the face of the abyss' at the beginning of Creation (Genesis 1:2). Another example: we think of the Holy Spirit as the Sanctifier, the One who makes holy the people of God, and yet it is obvious that the Father and the Son are also intimately involved in this process: Jesus has taught us to think of the Father as the source of forgiveness, something which is very important in the process of our sanctification, and again Jesus himself comes to us in the Sacrament of Holy Communion so that we may share in his risen life and be strengthened for our pilgrimage through life. This too is a vital part of that process of sanctification, which we sometimes seem to be assigning simply to the third Person of the Holy Trinity. God is three, Three Persons. But equally he is One, One God. We speak rightly of the 'Holy and undivided Trinity'.

So in thinking about God who has revealed himself as Trinity in Unity we have to do a kind of intellectual balancing act, holding together in our minds the Oneness and the Three-ness of God. In actual fact, however, the impossibility of doing this successfully, our sheer inability of understanding how One is Three and Three is One, serves to cut us down to size. We recognise in a most healthy and necessary way that God is beyond our ability to grasp and describe and label. We recognise, in fact, that God is God: the most profound of mysteries, 'the ground of our being', the One who is always beyond and above our human comprehension. The One who calls forth from us awe and reverence and worship, and who can only be known insofar as he chooses to reveal himself, and according to our limited ability to receive and assimilate that revelation.

God as the 'ground of all being', the Maker and Sustainer of all that is, is clearly at the centre of everything. Consequently, the doctrine of the Holy Trinity – that marvellous insight which God has given us into his very Nature and Being – lies at the heart of Christian belief. Because it is so central it needs to be kept before the Christian, which is one reason why it is customary to begin all prayer, both private and public, with the words 'In the Name of the Father, and of the Son, and of the Holy Spirit'. Followers of the Christian religion are before all else Trinitarian people. And this not simply because of a certain doctrine to which they give assent, but because as baptised people they are living within the life and being of the Holy Trinity. This cannot be otherwise, since the Christian believes that God the Father – in association with the Son and the Spirit – is constantly making and sustaining the individual; since God the Son – in association with the Father and the Spirit – is constantly in the process of applying his work of Redemption to him; and since God the Holy Spirit – in association with the Father and the Son – is constantly enlivening, renewing and sanctifying the Christian. The words with which the Christian is baptised 'I baptise you in the Name of the Father, and of the Son, and of the Holy Spirit' constitute no mere ritualistic formula. They refer to a profound and living truth. The Christian believes that he is living even now within the life of God who is Trinity in Unity, and that he will come to share ever more fully in that life as his redemption comes to fruition in the fulness of time.

7

'We believe in one holy catholic and apostolic Church . . .'

We have seen that in thinking and talking about God we are helped by pictures and models, by saying 'God is like . . .'. The models of Fatherhood and Kingship help us to think about the First Person of the Holy Trinity, whilst those of Fire and Wind and the Dove help us to think about God the Holy Spirit. As regards the Son, Our Lord Jesus Christ, we have those models which St John records: 'I am the Good Shepherd', 'I am the Bread of Life', 'I am the True Vine'. Just as models or pictures can help us in thinking about God, so they can also help us in thinking about the Church, and especially helpful is that picture which St Paul gives us in his first letter to the Corinthians. There he wrote 'Christ is like a single body, with its many limbs and organs . . . You are Christ's body, and each of you is like an organ of it (1 Cor. 12:12). We are so familiar with references to the Church as 'The Body of Christ' that the impact of these words is largely lost to us. What we are doing when we use them is using an analogy: we are saying 'The Church is like . . .' The Church is like a human body: a body in which Christ is the head (we might alternatively say the heart) and we are the arms and legs and other parts. It is an odd analogy to choose, although its oddness like its impact has been somewhat lost by over-familarity. Just what is this picture saying about the Church? How is the Church like a human body?

To begin with, the human body is a living thing, with its limbs dependent upon the life which flows into them. Cut off from the body, the arms and legs wither and die. Likewise, the Christian is dependent for life upon the Christ, for it is his resurrection life which animates the Church and its individual members. This life, which is His own risen life, flows into the

24

Christian at his baptism, which is why the Church is the sum of all those who have been baptised. It is made up of those people to whom Christ's life has come at baptism, and in whom that life has been nourished and strengthened by the regular reception of that other great sacrament, the sacrament of Holy Communion.

Further, the human body to which St Paul likens the Church is constantly changing. Its constituents are growing, decaying, being replaced. The Church is changing too, as new members are born into it by baptism; as members reach the end of their mortal life and are translated to that major part of the Church which is in heaven; and changing too as those within the fellowship of the Church are renewed, cleansed, transformed, by the work of the life-giving and sanctifying Spirit. The Church is never, in any dull and stultifying sense, constant; like the human body it is ever changing and developing. Then again, as in the human body, the members which make up the body of the Church are not independent but interdependent. Each of the many parts of the body is different, but together they make up the perfect whole. No one, we believe, is called upon to be a Christian in isolation. It is a corporate affair. We need our fellow members of the body of Christ, and they need us. We depend upon each other as we seek to grow into the likeness of Christ. None of us is called upon to give a solo performance. Each of us has a solemn and individual duty to support and encourage our fellow Christians, just as each member of the body has individual gifts and abilities to bring to the whole so that it is enriched and strengthened. The Christian has to recognise that if he fails to play his part in the worship, witness and service of the Church, then the whole is weakened by just that amount.

The Church is like a body, and we recognise a particular body, we identify it, by its characteristics: brown hair, bald head, big ears, etc. What are the distinguishing characteristics of the Church? The Creed lists four of them: The Church is One, Holy, Catholic and Apostolic. One? 'Nonsense', someone will say, 'It's split into any number of sub-churches and sects'. It is, and yet its Oneness is more fundamental than its disunity. It is One because all Christians worship One God, and broadly confess One Faith concerning him. It is One because Christians become members of the Church by one Baptism, through which they become participants in the resurrection life of the one Christ, and are enlivened by the indwelling of the one Spirit. But if the oneness of the Church is not immediately obvious to the observer, still less obvious in that second characteristic of the Church, holiness. It is manifest in those rare individual members of the Church who are named as Saints, but is holiness to be found in the body as a whole? Many members may indeed be far from holy as individuals, and yet the Church is Holy. Its holiness comes from its Head, into whose likeness its members are striving to grow, and from the Spirit who is holy and who is present and active in their lives, for he is the sanctifying Spirit.

One, Holy, and also Catholic. A word which means universal, but which has a richer meaning than world-wide. For the Kingdom of God crosses the boundaries of time no less than those of space. The present Church on earth is but a fragment of the whole, and similarly every local or national manifestation of the Church is only part of something greater. Finally, the Church is Apostolic. Apostolic as regards both its Faith and its Ordained Ministry. The word Apostle means 'witness'; the apostles of Jesus were witnesses to his life-giving words and actions and to his Resurrection. Witnesses to the Truth revealed by God, that Truth which the Church is to guard, treasure and proclaim in every century and place. Like that Truth, the Ordained Ministry of the Church has, we believe, been transmitted from the Apostles. A three-fold ministry of bishop, priest and deacon, each order having its distinctive function within the life of the body. The bishop who has the distinctive function of governing, leading, teaching, and ordaining; the priest who has a ministry centred upon the provision of pastoral care of those for whom the priest celebrates the Eucharist, pronounces Absolution, and gives Blessings; the deacon with a distinctive ministry of serving in many and various ways the People of God. This three-fold ministry emerged and was established in the first age of the Church, sometimes called the Apostolic Age, under the guidance of the Holy Spirit, and is vested with that authority given by Christ to his Apostles. It is a ministry which is an extension of the ministry of Christ himself, and through which he guides, feeds, builds-up, and unites the Church which he has founded.

In conclusion, it might be asked what in essence the Church is. One answer to this question is that the Church is that section of humanity which is being restored to what God intended all humanity to be. Humankind restored to unity with God, and to that eternal life for which men and women were designed. It is that part of humankind which has responded and is responding to God's loving initiative, his initiative in answering humanity's two-fold need for knowledge of God and reconciliation with him. In making this response, the Church is seeking to live by those two great commandments which our Lord has given: Love God – this is the first and great commandment, and the keeping of it involves the Church in the work of worship above all else, which is its primary function; Love your neighbour – that involves the Church in the proclamation of the good news of the Gospel. For the Christian believes that the very best thing he or she can do for a neighbour, the most precious gift which can be given to him or her, is the sharing of those life-giving truths which together constitute the Christian Faith.

8

'We acknowledge one baptism for the forgiveness of sins . . .'

In thinking about the Church we have already referred to Baptism, since it is through baptism that we become part of the One Holy Catholic and Apostolic Church. In baptism, Christians believe, our Lord Jesus Christ shares his resurrection life with the Christian: this new life flows into him, and the Christian becomes, according to Paul's strange metaphor, a 'limb' of the Body of Christ. The Church is the sum of those who have been incorporated into Christ in this way; of those who have been brought to new life in him by the Sacrament of Holy Baptism. Now a Sacrament is God's bestowel of some spiritual gift, with the invisible gift being given under some outward and visible sign. There are seven Sacraments, of which Baptism is the first, and in baptism the outward and visible sign is Water. Water poured out, water which speaks eloquently of the new life which is bestowed in baptism. For on the natural plane water is life-giving: animal and vegetable life is utterly dependent upon it. The same is true on the supernatural or spiritual plane: without the new life, the life of Christ which is given in baptism we have only natural, mortal life, which is limited both in its quality and in its duration. By contrast that eternal life given in baptism is eternal: it is without ending, and it has a fulness and richness which makes it different in kind from the life which is merely mortal.

Water, which is as we say, the 'matter' of the Sacrament of Baptism, speaks of life and of the means of growth. But water also speaks by virtue of its nature and its common use of cleansing, and in the context of the Holy Baptism it reminds us that in this Sacrament the Christian receives the washing away of sin. In association with the giving of new life and the giving of the Holy Spirit, whose Temple we become by baptism, there is a total cleansing from the effects of sin. A trinity of gifts in fact: the life of Christ, the indwelling of the Holy Spirit, and cleansing from sin – and yet these gifts are as intimately related and as inseparable as are the Persons of the Holy Trinity. 'One Baptism for the forgiveness of sins': despite this statement in the Creed, the baptismal gift of cleansing from sin tends to be somewhat overlooked in much discussion of baptism; we tend to speak more about sharing in the life of Christ and of the coming of the Spirit. This partial neglect of the forgiveness of sins which baptism gives is probably due to the fact that whilst adult baptism – in which the candidate personally rejects evil and turns to Christ – has remained the norm in theory, infant baptism has for many centuries been the norm in practice. And when someone is baptised maybe in early infancy, the gift of forgiveness of sin seems to be less real and less vital.

Yet even when baptism is administered in infancy, and before the candidate has reached that stage in his or her mental development when it is possible to recognise wrong and so commit sin by choosing it, even then the gift of forgiveness, the 'remission of sins', is given in the sacrament of baptism. For there are two kinds of sin, which in Christian thinking are called Actual Sin and Original Sin. Actual sin is that which the individual commits himself or herself, whenever the bad is chosen in preference to the good, and the person breaks in some particular one of those all-embracing commandments which Jesus gives to his disciples – 'Love God' and 'Love your neighbour'. All sin is a failure to adhere to those command- ments. As for original sin, this is inherited sin. It is our sharing, from very conception (or 'origin') in that whole disboedience, that general rebellion, in which the entire human race has been engaged throughout history, disobeying God and falling short of that perfect union with him – morally no less than spiritually – for which humanity was created. A shared fallenness, which leaves all mankind scarred and cut off from the Source of life and light. This sharing in the general darkness and disobedience of mankind is what we call Original Sin, and we need to be cleansed from this before we can begin to grow in the knowledge and likeness of Christ. In baptism, we believe that we are cleansed not only from those sins which we have knowingly committed on our own account, but also from this general taint of original sin. So that even when a person is baptised as a baby, the gift of cleansing, absolution, is given, and baptism does indeed bring the 'forgiveness of sins' to all who undergo it.

'We acknowledge one Baptism for the forgiveness of sins': there is one, common, baptism within the Christian Church, but also there is just one baptism for each member of the Church. For this Sacrament, unlike that of Holy Communion, can only be received once, once and for all. We are cleansed from sin in baptism, and yet like clothes, floors, and bodies we get dirty again. Baptism brings forgiveness for sins past, but it does not provide us with immunity from falling into disobedience in the future. Our freewill remains, and whilst it does so we can and will choose again what is wrong. So can our baptismal purity and freedom be regained? And if so, how? This was a question which exercised Christians in the early centuries, and some were of the opinion that the only answer was to delay baptism until the moment of death, so as to reach death with baptismal integrity unimpaired! But clearly this was not the answer to the dilemma. There must be another.

That answer is to be found in St John's Gospel. It is there that we learn the necessity of baptism, when Jesus in conversation with Nicodemus declares that 'In truth, I tell you, no one can enter the kingdom of God without being born from water and spirit (John 3:5). It is in this same Gospel that Jesus is recorded as saying to the apostles after his resurrection 'If you forgive any man sins, they stand forgiven' (John 20:23). At the Last Supper, Jesus had entrusted to the ministry of his Church the authority to act on his behalf and in his name in the taking, blessing, and sharing of the Bread and the Cup; here, before his ascension, he gave the ordained ministry of his Church a further responsibility and authority, that of pronouncing the forgiveness of sins in his name. Only God, of course, can forgive sin; only God, God the Son, can become present in Bread and Wine. But in both of these ministries Jesus had chosen to act through the priesthood which he instituted in his Church, and which has its foundation in the commands and in the authority given to the apostles. Through the mouth of that ministry he speaks his gracious words 'This is my Body, This is my Blood', and no less he speaks the words 'I absolve you from all your sins'. So whenever the priest says publicly in the Eucharist, or privately in the Confessional 'Almightly God have mercy upon you, pardon and deliver you from all your sins', he is exercising this ministry which Jesus himself has set up in his Church so that sins may be forgiven.

'You shall forgive seventy times seven' Jesus said to the man who asked him 'Shall I forgive my brother as many as seven times?' (Matthew 18: 21–22). Likewise God forgives us, over and over again, when we are genuinely sorry for the wrong we have done, and truly wish to make a new beginning. He wipes the slate clean, and in his infinite mercy and love he lets us become once more as we were at the moment of our baptism. By absolution, our baptismal state of freedom from sin is restored to us.

9

'We look for the resurrection of the dead . . .'

'We look for' – that is, we look forward to and expect – 'the resurrection of the dead'. Whose resurrection? Not that of Jesus, because his resurrection took place on the first Easter Day, and so we can hardly be 'looking forward' to that. No, not the resurrection of Christ, but the resurrection of all who have died in Christ, having been made one with him by Holy Baptism. This is what we 'look for'; this is our hope for the future. Resurrection for ourselves, and for all others who have died in Christ in the past, and who will die in Christ in the future. The teaching of the Church regarding our future state – that is the doctrine of the resurrection from the dead – is distinctive. It is no vague belief in the survival of some indefinable spiritual part of the individual. Jesus promised resurrection, St Paul elucidated that promise, the Creed asserts it, and the Church has taught it all down the centuries. Yet arguably it is the least understood of Christian teachings, and when it is taught many find it surprising, slightly shocking, and even unacceptable.

What is this teaching? The words of an Easter carol written at the end of the last century state it very simply:

My flesh in hope shall rest, And for a season slumber
'Till trump from east to west, shall wake the dead in number.*

This is the belief that on the Last Day, when Christ comes in glory, he will take the dust and ashes to which our mortal body has been reduced, and from those elements will fashion for us a new spiritual body, to which our soul will be rejoined, and in which we will then enter into the fulness of eternal life.

* *New English Hymnal* 121

At the moment of death, our soul – which can perhaps best be thought of in terms of 'personality', 'character', that which is more than our body, and which is so obviously missing from a corpse – our soul passes into God's keeping. As for our body, this is lain aside and is subject to decay. Or, as writers from the first century onward have expressed it, the body 'sleeps': 'My flesh in hope shall rest, And for a season slumber'. This is more than sentiment: 'sleep' is a good image because it suggests an eventual re-awakening: that re-awakening which is resurrection, the resurrection of the dead. But whilst resurrection is a re-awakening, it is much more than that. It is re-creation – more than mere reconstitution – it is transformation and transfiguration. These are the kind of words we have to use to express that last and greatest of all miracles, to which the Christian looks forward. For we shall not be as we have been; resurrection is far from being mere resuscitation, even if that were possible. The Christian believes that in the resurrection the body will be made perfect, made glorious: it will be subject no longer to change, pain, and decay. As an anonymous fifteenth-century writer declared:

> *O how glorious and resplendent*
> *Fragile body, shall thou be,*
> *When endued with so much beauty,*
> *Full of health, and strong and free,*
> *Full of vigour, full of pleasure*
> *That shall last eternally.**

To put it most simply, and indeed to get to the heart of the matter, the Christian believes that what happened to Jesus on the first Easter Day is going to happen to him or to her. Jesus died, and we shall die. He rose, and we shall rise. His body was resurrected, not resuscitated: it was transformed and glorified; our bodies likewise will be resurrected on the Last Day. This follows from the fact that we have been joined to Christ at

---

* *New English Hymnal* 401

baptism, and that we are living and growing in Christ as we live out the sacramental life. We are 'in Christ', made limbs of that body of which he is head. Christ is risen, we shall rise. What happen to the Head must happen to the body.

Now, if that resurrection of the dead which we look for is going to be the same in kind as the resurrection of Jesus, then we can learn about our resurrection body by looking at his: by looking at that body of Jesus which left the sepulchre on Easter Day and which was seen and touched by his disciples during the forty days which ended with his ascension into heaven. For the risen body of Christ is the prototype for our resurrection body. When we do this, two things are apparent: that there were similarities, points of contact, between the mortal body taken of Mary and the resurrection body, and also that there were differences. We note that the disciples could indeed see and touch the risen Lord, and that he could eat and speak and move. Furthermore his body displayed the wounds inflicted in the course of his Passion (Luke 24:38). There was nothing shadowy, ethereal or unreal about the risen body – it was truly him and his. But at the same time it was different. The risen body of Christ was free from ordinary physical limitations. He could apparently appear and disappear at will, and again, some of his disciples did not immediately recognise him. The same body, and yet different. Real, substantial, but at the same time having a new quality and dimension. We learn from it what we in our turn will be like at that General Resurrection which we 'look for'. It will be us, but made glorious. The identity between our mortal and our resurrection body will be ensured by the fact that is is the fragments of our present body which form as it were the stuff from which our new body will be fashioned. We will be a new creation. But the vital, and the necessary link if that new body is truly to be 'us' will be there. On that last Easter Day our graves will be empty, just as the sepulchre of Jesus was empty on the first Easter Day. And for the same reason: because the miracle of resurrection will have taken place.

Now the importance of this teaching lies first in the fact that it is Truth: part of that body of truth which has been revealed to us, and which is a disclosure of God's Nature and Purpose. But this particular doctrine has a further importance in that it makes four significant affirmations. First, it is an affirmation of our essential nature as God created it: an affirmation of our twofold being, the body which is physical, and the soul which is spiritual. Neither part – body or soul – is unimportant, inferior, or, ultimately, dispensable. By the personal pronouns 'you', 'us', 'me', we refer to that unity of body and soul which we are. 'Me' does not refer to my soul in isolation, and if only my soul, that one part of me, is to inherit eternal life, it would be questionable as to whether it makes any sense to speak about 'me' being saved. Second, this doctrine of the resurrection of the dead affirms the essential goodness of the material order. The body is not something inferior, to be permanently abandoned and disposed of at death, whilst only a 'higher' part of us has a future. No, the body itself has a future. It will be taken and re-created at the Last Day. It is no mere throwaway container for the soul. Third, the doctrine of the resurrection of the dead affirms the completeness, the all-embracing character of Christ's saving work. The whole Christ rose from the dead, the tomb was empty. Jesus does not just salvage souls, he saves whole people. Our body is to be redeemed no less than our soul. There is nothing limited or partial about Christ's saving work. Fourth, and finally, this doctrine affirms the fact and the consequences of our incorporation into Christ. The fact that we are made one with him by baptism is both the foundation of the teaching of resurrection, and is also affirmed by it. By baptism we are already 'in Christ'; by the spiritual and sacramental life we are growing in Christ; the flowering of this life in Christ will be our resurrection. In that, our redemption will reach its glorious conclusion, and we will be 'like him' for ever.

10

'and the life of the world to come.'

When we contemplate our future hope at the conclusion of the Creed, we make two statements, one rather general, the other more specific. The more specific statement is about resurrection 'We look for the resurrection of the dead'. Here is one element in our future hope about which we can be definite. We believe that on the Last Day our body, which has been reduced to dust and ashes, will be re-created and made glorious, and that our soul will be reunited with it. How can we be specific about this one part of our hope for the future? Simply because the Church, in the person of the Apostles, has had firsthand experience of a resurrection body, namely the body of Jesus. In the risen Christ we have seen how we shall be on the Last Day, the day of the General Resurrection. Christ is the prototype, or 'first-fruits' as St Paul puts it. So we know, at least, what resurrection is. But this is the one and only aspect of its future life about which the Church on earth already has firsthand experience. Which is why that other statement in the Creed about our future has to be general: 'and the life of the world to come'.

In the Gospels Jesus says comparatively little about heaven. Various explanations are advanced for this, the most satisfactory of which is the fact that we are probably incapable of understanding very much about 'the life of the world to come'. Because it will be so completely different from life in this world, there is nothing in our experience to which our life in the next world can be compared. Essentially, the Christian accepts the fact of heaven, the life of the world to come, on the basis of our Lord's promise, and also as something which is consequent upon the love which God has declared himself to have towards his people. As a loving Father, his will is that our end should be happiness which is complete and without ending.

But can we do anything more than state our expectation of heaven, and our belief that we will enjoy it as resurrected people? Or is all else an impenetrable mystery? The Christian would say that whereas the future life must remain mysterious, we have nonetheless certain insights regarding it: insights or convictions which are of a general character, but which do give some kind of framework for our thinking in this area of belief. The first of these insights is that there must surely be a period of preparation before we enter into the fulness of the life to come. This is a matter for realism as much as for humility. Few people indeed would seem to be ready at the moment of death to enter into the presence of God; indeed only those who have attained exceptional sanctity, so that they are recognisable as saints. Most of us will not die in that state, and will need a time of preparation. Sometimes this time of preparation for entering into the presence of God is called Purgatory, although that term has overtones of punishment which most Christians would wish to reject. The time of preparation is best thought of not in terms of punishment so much as purification, or polishing. A place in which we are made ready so that we are not shrivelled-up when we come to behold God in his majesty and perfection. There are some, of course, who claim that the Redemption which Christ has accomplished and upon which we have laid-hold by faith and by sacramental grace, make this preparation unnecessary, but this does not seem to be realistic. We might imagine that we have fallen into a deep and muddy pond in the garden. We have been rescued – someone has pulled us out and thereby saved our life. We are no longer in danger – we have been saved. But despite this, we are as yet in no state to walk straight into the drawingroom for afternoon tea. We need some cleaning-down and re-clothing before we are ready for that. Just so, most Christians believe that 'the life of the world to come' will be preceded after death by some kind of preparation, a continuation of the process of sanctification which has been begun in this present life. And further, that whilst this process is continuing, the departed can be assisted by prayers offered by the church here on earth.

The next insight or conviction which might be mentioned has been touched on already: that whatever else heaven is, it will be a coming-into and rejoicing-in the presence of God. A state of nearness to God, a beholding of his glory, and consequently a being 'lost in wonder, love and praise'. A 'being-with' God which for our part we cannot fully experience in this life, even though for his part God is truly and absolutely with us all the time, here and now. So that heaven can be said to be an opening of our eyes — the attainement and perpetual enjoyment of the Vision of God. Seeing face to face as the clouds part and as the veil is withdrawn; experiencing God in such a way that we are filled with endless and unimaginable delight. Essentially a 'being-with' God, who is the source of all true joy and goodness.

'Lost in wonder, love and praise': here is a further insight or conviction: that our chief activity and delight in heaven will be praise. A joining with the holy angels in their characteristic work of giving glory to God. This will be the perfection of our loving of God, since worship is essentially the exercise of love. Unlike our worship her on earth, our worship in heaven will be spontaneous and natural: an unforced response to God as he is and as we shall see him. The Christian, we believe, will be unable to tear him or herself away from the vision of God, because it will be so full of wonder and beauty. As Fr Faber wrote in a humn:

> *What rapture will it be*
> *Prostrate before thy throne to lie,*
> *And gaze and gaze on thee**

'We believe in the life of the world to come'. A fulness of life for which we will need preparation; a life where we will behold the glory of God; a life in which that vision will be a source of deep and unending joy to us, and which will call forth from us spontaneous and unceasing worship. This is our

---

* *New English Hymnal* 410

Christian hope: life in the new Jerusalem, which for the Christian is the goal of our pilgrimage, the object which we are
striving to achieve. We believe that God made man so that this
may be attained: life in his presence, basking in the warmth of
that love which he has for every person whom he has brought
into being. A love, furthermore, which in heaven we will be
able to return. The recognition of this goal, and the awareness
of that 'life of the world to come' enables the Christian to see
this present life in perspective and proportion. The Christian is
able to comprehend that life on earth is nothing more – and
nothing less – than a preparation for the life of heaven which
is to come. Because it is nothing more than this, we must not
look for or expect full and established joy and peace here on
earth. And because this present life is nothing less than a
preparation for heaven, the Christian must not fail to use the
time and opportunity which he has for winning the heavenly
Jerusalem and the joys which it holds. Only if this life is seen
as a prelude for heaven, and as a chance to win it, will the
Christian live rightly and purposefully. The Christian rever-
ences and enjoys this mortal life, and the world in which it is
lived-out. But always there is a looking forward to 'the life of
the world to come'. It is upon that that the sights of the
Christian are set.

PART TWO

Christian Living

CHRISTIAN LIVING

(*The Commandments, from The Order for Holy Communion Rite A (Appendix 78B), in The
Alternative Service Book 1980, Copyright the Central Board of Finance of the Church of England*)

1

'I am the Lord your God. You shall have no other gods before me'

To have thought about Christian belief before thinking about Christian living is to have got things in the correct order. Simply because the moral code which forms part of the Christian religion is firmly based upon the beliefs which Christians hold. That code is based upon what we believe about God, and one of the things which we believe about God is that he brought us into being out of love. This being so, it follows that he wants us to be happy, and so like any good parent who desires the safety and happiness of his child, God makes rules for us: he gives us directions concerning our behaviour. Not out of awkwardness, or the wish to make our lives complicated; love is the reason why God gives us commandments, so that we may do these things which make for happiness and avoid those things which make for misery. Love is also the means by which those commandments are fulfilled, for Jesus has taught us that the Commandments can be summed up in two basic principles for action: love God and love your neighbour. So it is that 'Love is the fulfilling of the Law' (Romans 13:10).

So the principles which govern the behaviour of the Christian – his moral code – are given by God. Those principles form part of the Revelation which God has given to his people. Hence our Christian moral code is based upon our Christian belief; it is no man-made morality, founded upon what man himself considers to be expedient and convenient. The rules governing Christian behaviour come from God, and to God we owe obedience. But in obeying God by living as he has taught us to live, we express our love for him; love for the God who himself gives us commandments out of love.

'You shall have no other gods before me': here in the first of the Ten Commandments, God the Lawgiver asserts the place which is rightly his in our lives. This truth is fundamental to Christian living; it is a basic fact about our relationship with God. He is Lord, and the obeying and loving of him must be at the centre of the disciple's thinking, speaking, and action. All that the Christian does must be done from the wish to conform to his revealed will, and be inspired by the desire to love and serve him.

But why should God had this primacy in our lives? Why should we choose – because he has certainly given us the ability and the opportunity to choose – why should we choose to fashion every part of our living in accordance with those commandments by which the divine will is expressed? First, because God made us and we are his. He brought us into being and we belong to him. This in itself makes it right that we should obey him; the fact of his ownership gives him claim over us. This factor is very clearly founded upon Christian belief, the belief that God is Creator. But another factor is based on experience, namely that we discover by experience that the principles which God gives us to direct our action are indeed good; their rightness and his wisdom are attested to by the fact that those principles for action do in fact make for happiness and peace, both in society and in the lives of individuals. But thirdly, and primarily, the Christian holds that God has claim upon our obedience in regard to how we live because of the depths of the love which he has shown for us, above all in the saving work of Jesus Christ, and in the continued outpouring of his gifts upon the Church and upon its individual members. As creator, as source of wisdom, and as the God who loves us in an unconditional and costly way, he has claim to be at the centre of our lives, the one whom the disciple seeks to follow joyfully and willingly in every part of his living.

'I am the Lord your God. You shall have no other gods before me'. The demands which God makes upon us, and which as disciples of Jesus we accept, are all-embracing. They concern every part and area of our life. Just as the Christian is seeking to live more and more in awareness of the presence of God, so too he is seeking to conform each and every action, thought, word, ambition and hope to the will of God; to the will of God as revealed to his ancient people in the Ten Commandments, and as summarised so simply and yet in so absolute a way by Our Lord in the two principles that we should love God and our neighbour (Mark 12:28–31). For all Christian morality, all Christian teaching about our mental and physical behaviour, is simply a working-out in practical terms of these two guiding principles which summarise the more ancient commandments. The two principles spelt out by Jesus cover every situation in which the Christian may be placed. Sometimes, of course, it is easier than at other times to see what loving God and loving your neighbour demands of us in a particular occurrence of our daily life. But always with prayer, reflection, and perhaps wise advice it is possible to find the right and genuinely loving response. We discover God's will for us by applying and working-out the two basic principles, and then by seeking to act in accordance with his will. Then we are in fact seeking to have God at the centre of our life as Lord, which in turn is to obey his commandment that we should have no other gods before him. For this commandment is about giving God his proper place as the One who is Lord and Master, Father and Creator. In each situation the Christian must learn to ask 'what does God want me to do, say, think?'; which is asking 'what is most compatible with loving God and my neighbour in this situation in which I find myself?'

The first commandment speaks of the place which belongs to God in our Christian living; of how we must enthrone him as Lord of our lives, letting his revealed will be the springboard and inspiration of all that we do and are. The Christian must have no other gods before him; obedience to God must not be just occasional, when it is convenient or when he or she remembers. God gives all, and he demands all. He says without qualification 'I am the Lord your God. You must have no other gods before'.

2

'You shall not make for yourself a graven image . . . You shall not bow down to them or worship them'

If the first commandment warns us against giving God a subordinate, a less-than-central place in our lives, then the second warns us against losing sight of God entirely through replacing him with an idol. But in doing this, the second commandment also draws our attention to a fact about our human nature: the fact that God has made us with a built-in need to pursue some aim, to strive after something and seek to attain it, indeed to serve something and bow down before it. The need, in fact, for some kind of god. Admittedly it is a need which it is difficult to define and pin down, and one which remains unrecognised and unspoken by most people, hidden in the subconscious. Yet this need to strive and to attain, this commitment to some purpose which we might call the 'Ultimate Concern' of each individual, would seem to be universal. The object of this striving may be as high as God, or as low as the mere gratification of our animal senses and instincts. The tendency is there, a part of our make-up.

Part of our make-up and so, the Christian would say, something which has been implanted by God, and so is in itself good, however much and however often man chooses what is less than God as the object of his ultimate concern. A thirst in man which God intends to be a thirst for him, the One who, when found, can give that fulness of life and joy which all men seek after. We believe that God made us out of love, in order that we might be loved by him, and might return his love. This is our God-given purpose: the finding, possessing, and loving of God. God alone, the Christian believes, is the worthy object of a man's search and man's worship. He has created man with

48

a longing for happiness and fulfilment, and with the desire to fall down before its Source. God himself is the answer to that need and to that longing which he has implanted in man.

Yet too easily man fastens upon something which is less than God, and makes that thing his ultimate concern. Too easily we dis-direct our striving, and seek for and worship what is no less than an idol. At the time when the Ten Commandments were given, men literally carved images and worshipped them. Indeed, whilst Moses was on Sinai receiving the commandments from God, the people of Israel were making and worshipping a golden calf at the feet of the mountain (Exodus 32:1–6). Today in the western world the idols which men and women set up are more sophisticated than golden calves, and yet mankind has lost none of its capacity for setting up alternative gods and falling down before them. What kind of graven images are made today to be the ultimate concerns of some people? It is not difficult to list some of the most popular alternatives to God. Perhaps materialism is the most obvious: the striving for and the holding of wealth and possession, the getting of things. This is a concentration upon material things which have no power of themselves to bring peace of mind and happiness, and so are unworthy to be set up as objects of ultimate concern. Also in the pantheon of false gods we find the seeking and possessing of power and influence, the desire to dominate, control, and manipulate the lives and careers of other people. Some make the acquisition and wielding of these the chief aim of their lives. Then again, others seek and treasure social standing and success: popularity, being admired and envied; these too can be made matters of ultimate concern. Again, the pantheon also contains that crude god whose followers seek merely to gratify their bodily cravings. These make the procurement and enjoyment of sex, drink or food – or even just comfort and luxury – the chief aim of their lives.

It may be objected that none of the things which have just been listed as possible false gods – wealth, possession, power, influence, popularity, success, sex, food and drink – none of these things is wrong or evil in itself. That is true. It is when any of these things is made into a god, made into a matter of ultimate concern, that the second commandment is broken. When this happens, what should be the servant is in fact served, and those who mistake the creature for the creator are set upon a road which can only lead to disappointment and emptiness. It is to risk being left with a handful of dust rather than with a crown of eternal life.

The first and second commandments 'You shall have no other gods before me', and 'You shall not make for yourselves a graven image', go together. They speak in general, but in fundamental, terms about the foundation upon which the life of the Christian is to be built and upon which all his or her actions and attitudes are to be founded. The Christian believes that if he is to act wisely, justly and rightly, then he must set God and God alone at the centre of his life, and make the serving and the loving of God his ultimate concern. For he is a 'jealous God', who will not share his glory with another. He is also, though, the God who shows 'steadfast love to thousands of those who love him and keep his commandments'.

3

'You shall not take the name of the Lord your God in vain'

Some of the commandments refer to very specific actions: 'You shall not steal', 'You shall not commit adultery', 'You shall not covet your neighbour's possessions', and just because the reference of these commandments seems narrow it could be thought that their significance for the daily life of the Christian is proportionately limited. But in actual fact those commandments which seem to relate to very particular actions and situations embody fundamental and far-reaching principles. The third commandment is a case in point. 'You shall not take the Name of the Lord your God in vain': superficially, this commandment seems to do no more than warn the Christian against using the word 'God', the holy name of Jesus, and the title 'Christ' in a casual and blasphemous way. The commandment certainly does condemn that kind of usage, and the condemnation it makes was reinforced by Jesus when he commanded his followers not to swear by earth, heaven, or Jerusalem (Matthew 5:34–37). But the third commandment does much more than condemn a type of verbal usage which both Jews and Christians find distasteful and offensive. The commandment speaks to us about our whole attitude towards the God who should, in accordance with the first and second commandments, be at the very centre of our life and thinking.

What is the message of this commandment for those who are seeking to live the Christian life? Quite simply that our attitude towards God should be marked by reverence: reverence, awe, 'the spirit of holy fear'. It is the opposite to thinking and speaking about God in a casual, flippant way, as if he was our next-door neighbour rather than our creator. The commandment seems to be directed to modes of speaking, but its reference is wider than this; it is about the whole attitude of

51

the Christian. Further, the reverence which it enjoins is closely bound up with the loving of God: love makes us bristle when someone very close to us is spoken of in a disrespectful and flippant way. It is to do with the loving of God, which is something to engage our heart and mind and soul, and it is associated with that courtesy and humility which have a part in love.

So the third commandment concerns reverence, and its message seems one which is necessary and urgent for the Church and world of today, where so often the spirit of reverence seems to be forgotten. Why should this be? Perhaps one reason is to be found in the fact that western society flushed with success in the field of scientific advance and achievement, is in a mood of self-confidence, a self-confidence which is not very conducive to the attitude of reverence. Again in the religious sphere, the contemporary climate of questioning, reducing, re-interpreting the truths of the Christian faith, this too produces a milieu in which the spirit of holy fear finds it difficult to flourish. Furthermore, some would argue that the rather mundane language of contemporary liturgy and the trend towards informality in worship, does little to build up an atmosphere in which an attitude of reverence is promoted and developed. But whatever the causes may be, it seems to be indisputable that the present generation of Christians is not noted for its reverential approach to God, and perhaps this is something which the Christian church needs to rediscover. Of course God is our Father and our friend, and we are his children, loved and cared for by him. But he is also our Creator and our Lord, the One before whole judgement throne we must ultimately come. We have to both find and preserve a balance between confidence and reverence in our approach to God: a balance in our public and private prayer which in turn permeates all of our thinking and speaking. There should be confidence insofar as we are children approaching a loving father, and reverence insofar as we are creatures confronted by the awesome holiness and mysterious 'otherness' of God.

The third commandment reminds us of the reverence we should have towards God himself, but we recall that all things belong to God, and just because they are his creation so they too deserve to be treated with reverence. The natural world is an obvious example. This, both as made by God and as being an expression of his glory is to be reverenced by mankind, whose role is to be steward and who must never degenerate into that of exploiter. To exploit the natural world is to be guilty of irreverence towards its creator. Again, what we sometimes refer to as 'the things of God', the things used in the course of Christian worship, these in a special way deserve to be treated with reverence through their association with the God whom we worship. But above all, we should reverence our fellow men and women, created in the divine image. To belittle, deride, scorn or oppress another human being is certainly to be guilty of irreverence, since Jesus has taught us that we are to recognise and serve him 'in the least of our brethren'. Our attitude towards God and towards all that he has made should properly be reverential. Hence it is inescapable that reverence is to be a mark or characteristic of the Christian in his everyday living and thinking.

Reverence for God and the things of God lies behind the third commandment 'You shall not take the Name of the Lord your God in vain', but so far no definition of reverence has been given. We have suggested that it is the opposite of being casual or flippant in our thinking or speaking about God, and it is also the opposite of self-assertiveness in the face of God. But essentially reverence is right judgement, a seeing of things as they truly are; a grasping of the worth, wonder, holiness and mystery of God, and the realisation that in comparison with God we are very small. This, followed by a readiness to give in an ample way 'honour where honour is due'.

4

'Remember the sabbath day, to keep it holy'

If a devout elderly lady was told that she had broken one of the Ten Commandments every week for the whole of her life, she would probably be indignant. But if reference was being made to the fourth commandment, 'Remember the Sabbath Day to keep it holy', the charge would most likely be correct. Because this is the one commandment which Christians are not required keep, bearing in mind that the Jewish Sabbath is something entirely different from the Christian Sunday. For Sabbath and Sunday really have nothing in common. They fall on different days of the week, they commemorate different events, and they are celebrated in different ways. During the past four hundred years there has been a tendency within Protestantism to identify Sunday with Sabbath – an attempt to regard them as essentially the same thing in such a way that all the prohibitions belonging to the Jewish Sabbath belong equally to the Christian Sunday. But such an attempt is misguided. Sunday is not 'The Christian Sabbath'; it is a specifically Christian institution which belongs wholly to the new dispensation rather than to the old.

Does it matter, then, that the Christian knowingly and consistently fails to observe the fourth commandment? Not at all. Does it matter, then, if he or she breaks any of the other nine? Most certainly. How can this be? The fact is that the fourth commandment is different in kind from its fellows, insofar as the other nine are based on what is called Natural Law whilst this one is not. By Natural Law we mean rights and wrongs which are so basic, so fundamental and generally accepted, that we might think of them as being implanted in the very nature of things – hence the name Natural Law. To kill, to steal, to fail to honour parents, these things are wrong everywhere and always, in every age and culture. They contravene laws which are neither made by mankind nor given by God through special revelation, but which can be worked out by the exercise of our God-given reason; they are rules governing behaviour which can be arrived at by all men and women of commonsense and goodwill. But the fourth commandment, 'Remember the Sabbath day to keep it holy', this is not based on Natural Law; rather it belongs to the ceremonial law of God's ancient people the Jews, and it could not have been worked out by unaided reason. As ceremonial law, it was given not by reason but by special revelation, as part of the Old Covenant which God made with his people. Hence for those who live under the New Covenant, under the Christian dispensation, it is no more binding than all the other specifically Jewish ceremonial laws concerning animal sacrifice, ritual purification, and whatever, which we find in the Old Testament of the Bible. So having made the devout elderly lady indignant, we should hasten to assure her that she has not done wrong in failing to observe the fourth commandment. For it is no more binding upon her and upon other Christians than are the ceremonial laws of Islam or Hindi.

Is the fourth commandment, therefore, totally irrevelant to the Christian, so that nothing would be lost if it was omitted from any reading or consideration of the Ten Commandments? By no means, for like the other commandments the fourth has enshrined within it an important principle for Christian living. This principle is that we have a duty to give back to God a proportion of the time which he has given to us. For we are to be stewards of our time, just as we are to be stewards of the natural world and its resources, and this involves using our time responsibly and wisely, since it is one of the most precious commodities which we have. In order to use our time wisely we must consider again what our purpose is – why it is that God has given us life and so given us time. Our purpose is to love God and win heaven, and so a proportion of our time must be set aside for the worship and the contemplation of

God. This, for the Christian, is both a solemn duty, a privilege and a joy, for he or she knows that God is himself the source of all peace and joy, and that it is in communion with him that his precious gifts are bestowed upon us. The fourth commandment reminds the Christian of the duty to set aside time for prayer and worship, and for the pursuit of the spiritual life. This part of that wise stewardship which God has entrusted to us.

But in the form in which it is given, the commandment 'Remember the Sabbath day, to keep it holy', goes further than merely reminding us that we should give of our time to God as we plan and live out our lives. It suggests, in mentioning the Sabbath day, that quite specific times should be set aside for spiritual things, that there should be some order and regularity in the living-out of this area of our lives. For Jesus in his incarnate life it was Saturday, the Sabbath, which was set aside as the day of the week when the worship of God would be the prime concern. The Church, in following its Master, has ever held to the principle of a particular day being set aside for the things of God. But for the Christian Church it is Sunday, the day of Christ's resurrection, which has been held special. In the Jewish religion Saturday, the Sabbath, is a weekly celebration of the day on which God rested when the work of creation was completed (Genesis 2:2–3); in the Christian religion we celebrate week by week the day on which Jesus rose victorious from the grave, thereby inaugurating the new creation. From the beginning of the Christian era, followers of our Lord Jesus Christ have seen it as appropriate in their stewardship of time to set aside some part of that day to gather together to celebrate the triumph of their Lord, and to do so by gathering together to celebrate the Eucharist in accordance with his command (1 Cor. 11:23–25). For there in bread and wine the Christ who is risen becomes present to his people to be their life and their strength; present as he was in those special meals at the time of his resurrection, in the upper room, at Emmaus, and on the shores of the lake. By this means the glorious resurrection of Christ is remembered, and the day of his rising is kept holy. Worship, it must always be remembered, lies at the heart of the life of the Christian and so Sunday – the primary day for the Eucharist – should lie at the heart of the Christian's week; ever since the first century, attendance at the Sunday Eucharist has been seen by the Church as a fundamental part of authentic Christian living.

All time belongs to God: we solemnly assert this fact at the blessing of the Easter Candle on Easter Eve, when we use the words 'All time belongs to him and all ages; to him be blessing and power through ever age and for ever'. The time which we have is God's gift, and a basic aim of the spiritual life which the Christian is seeking to live is the sanctification of all time by living more and more in a state of constant awareness of God's presence. Not having yet attained this aim of a constant state of recollection, however, we need to set aside certain times when we will be present to God by the practice of prayer and worship. Sunday worship in celebration of the risen Christ is an obvious setting aside of time for God. But this must be supported – as it will be nourished – by daily prayer, private prayer, and the Christian needs to have some personal rule or resolution about this too. The Christian aims to sanctify each day by the offering of prayer, the spending of time consciously in God's presence, this being in itself the very essence of prayer.

We sometimes use the word duty when we speak of prayer and worship; the duty which we have to give God our time in the giving to him of our attention. Yet essentially the fourth commandment and the principle which it brings before us is not about duty in any onerous and over-formal sense; rather it is about the loving of God. For by giving God our time in a regular and disciplined way we are fulfilling Jesus' commandment that we should love him 'with all our heart and soul and mind' (Matthew 22:37), and also we are enabling ourselves to grow in the love of God. Worship and prayer are about loving God, and it belongs to the very nature of love to be generous. Therefore the Christian asks 'Am I generous in the time I set aside for God each week and each day? Am I, by prayer and worship, making holy the time which God has given to me?'

5

'Honour your father and your mother'

The first four commandments concern our relationship with God; for the Christian this relationship is the foundation upon which his everyday life is built. The Christian knows that he is living in God's sight, and that his aim is to give glory to God in all that he does. The subject of the first four commandments reminds us that the loving of God must be our priority, and that we must be careful not to allow anything else to usurp the place which God properly has in our lives. We also learn that our whole attitude towards God is to be marked by reverence, and that we need to set aside specific times when we can develop our knowledge and love of God by prayer and worship. Jesus summarises the first four commandments in this charge that we should love God with all our heart, mind, and soul.

The subject of the other six commandments is our relationship with others. They concern men and women in society, men and women in their dealings with other people. For God has made us social creatures, able to find fulfilment not solely in relationship with him but also in relationship with one another. 'It is not good for man to be alone' (Genesis 2:18), and with the possible exception of those who have the unusual vocation to the solitary life as hermits, men and women are enriched immeasurably by their dealings one with another. These further commandments are likewise summarised by Jesus, in his charge that we should love our neighbour as ourself.

Since we originate in the relationship existing between our parents, it is appropriate that the first of these six commandments should concern our attitude towards them. The commandment tells us that our relationship with our parents is to be characterised by honour: 'Honour your father and mother' – respect them, hold them in high regard. Perhaps we may feel that the concepts of respect and honour sound somewhat cold and formal in regard to what is properly a very close and intimate relationship, and yet we remind ourselves that honour and respect, together with courtesy, patience, understanding and so on, are ingredients which go to make up that collective entity, love. But why is it especially important that the Christian should 'honour' his father and mother? Why is this particular aspect of love singled out? Ultimately because the good, responsible, loving parent serves to do nothing less than reveal the nature of God to the child – this is why honour is due. The Christian does of course teach the child about God in an explicit way; he or she tells the child at an important stage in its development about the things which God has done and is doing; the parent teaches the child also to worship and to pray. But any good, loving parent – whether Christian or not – reveals the very nature of God to a child in a way which is more fundamental still. This is because the relationship of the loving parent with the child is a mirror, a reflection, of the relationship which exists between God and every person whom he has brought into being. In the part which they play in the generation of the child, the parents 'share in the work of creation', as one of the new baptismal liturgies puts it. The parents feed the child, clothe it, protect it, forgive it, give it rules and principles for right action. They offer it sympathy, support, and understanding. The child can turn to them in sorrow or distress, knowing that it will find a ready ear and a generous heart. The parents see the best in the child, and they seek to bring out the best. Above all, their love is unconditional; it is not dependent upon the child's response, and not abated by any failure of the child to return love. In all this, the good parent both reflects and reveals the very nature of that love which God has for mankind, which is revealed in Jesus Christ, and which according to St John is the prime characteristic of God (1 John 4:8). Such indeed is the nature of this revelation and reflection that Jesus himself has taught us to use Fatherhood as a prime image in our thinking about God:

'Our Father' is the mode of address which has been given us to use in the Lord's Prayer. This, ultimately, is why the child's love for the parent should include the giving of honour: because the parent in his love for the child is revealing to it the wonder of the love of God.

When we consider the relationship of parent and child, the subject of the fifth commandment, it is natural that we should also consider the family unit within which that relationship is set. If, as we have said, the right relationship between parent and child is a reflection of the relationship between the Christian and God, then the broader relationship within the family – between brothers and sisters, grandparents and grandchildren, and so on – this should no less be a reflection of the relationships which rightly exist between those who have been joined together within the Christian Church through the re-birth of Holy Baptism. The parent/child relationship is given a special dignity because it speaks to us of the God/creature relationship; likewise our relationships within our human family are given a special dignity because they speak of the relationship which all Christians enjoy with one another within the body of Christ. We honour our parents because they reveal God to us in the love which they have towards us; we honour the members of our human family because they symbolise the family of the Church, of which we are also members.

The family, symbol of the Church, founded on the God-revealing parent/child relationship, and created by God as the basic unit in society, is held in honour by the Christian. He seeks to promote it by resisting whatever factors in society may tend to weaken, damage, or distort the family, and by encouraging conditions in society which will serve to protect and consolidate family life. One of the marriage rites of the Church reminds us that God instituted marriage partly so that children might grow up within the stable and secure setting of a united family, and so that husband and wife might likewise enjoy the stability which the family situation makes possible.

Yet again we remind ourselves that God, who was motivated by love in his creation of mankind, desires above all else that his creature should enjoy true and lasting happiness. The family is one means by which God's purpose is achieved, and in which the nature of God's love towards us can be disclosed. So Christians honour family life, just as they honour their father and mother. Both are of God, both reveal God. In seeking to give this honour, Christians seek in a particular way to obey the commandment that we should love one another; they seek to exercise that love which must characterise all of their relationships.

6

'You shall not kill'

You shall not kill: this commandment is terse, unqualified and direct. It is uncompromising, and it inevitably leads the Christian to take certain stances which are contrary to the accepted wisdom of a non-Christian society. You shall not kill, and so for the Christian euthanasia is wrong; abortion (in all but very special circumstances) is wrong; capital punishment is wrong; suicide is wrong; all these are contrary to this commandment and so, we believe, contrary to the will of God. This, like all of the commandments, makes demands upon us, and somehow the gravity of these demands seems to be underlined by the brevity and directness of the prohibition.

At its heart the sixth commandment is about respect for human life, life which we believe to be a precious and mysterious gift from God – or perhaps more truly something lent rather than forgiven. For ultimately since all life proceeds from God, so it belongs to him; it is not ours to end just as and when we think fit, so that neither society nor the individual is empowered to terminate human life at will. But this commandment concerns more than just the preservation of life: it is about respect for human beings, for persons. As life is not to be terminated upon human decision, so whoever possesses God's gift of life is to be accounted sacred, precious, and to be respected and valued. For each person is created in the divine image, made 'in the likeness of God' (Gen. 1:27), insofar as he or she shares in the divine attributes of rationality, creativity, and the capacity to enter into loving relationships. We have these gifts, and whether or not we recognise their origin and indeed their significance they nonetheless characterise us as being of God. In some people, of course – in the vandal, the rapist, the oppressor, the bully – the divine image is horribly distorted and undeveloped. Yet it is there indelibly, and every

63

sinner is potentially a saint. You shall not kill: life is from God, it belongs to God, and the possessor of it is made in God's image. Therefore to kill is to do nothing less than to destroy that which bears God's image, a thing which is therefore the grossest sacrilege and for the Christian, the ultimate and most terrible crime.

This commandment asserts the sanctity of life and, implicitly, the rights of those to whom this gift has been entrusted by the Creator. We humans are complex beings, reflecting the triune God who brought us into being in our threefold nature – body, mind, and spirit. Each of these aspects of the person has rights, which are to be honoured and respected by society and by its members. The body: it has a right to food and to proper medical care. The Christian knows himself to be his brother's keeper; we are responsible for one another. And so we can never be indifferent to the fact that there are many people in the world who are deprived of those things which the well-being of their bodies requires. God has given humanity the gift of food, and justice and love demand that this food should be shared amongst all people. The fact that many people in the world are starving implies that the sixth commandment is being broken. The mind: this too has rights. The right to education, so that the full potential of this gift from God may be realised, to his glory. Body, mind, and spirit: the spirit or 'soul' – the essential person, to be thought of maybe in terms of 'character' and 'personality', the part of us which has the capacity to relate to God – this element has the right for its deepest need to be met, the need for God. Hence the Christian believes that the Christian faith, the truth revealed by God together with the means of union with God – that these should be available to all people, so that the soul may find in God its eternal purpose and joy. All people, we believe, have the right to hear the good news of the Gospel, to receive the Faith, and to be united in the fellowship of all God's people.

We have been thinking of the rights which all human

beings enjoy, and of how a proper respect for our common humanity, made in God's image, demands that these rights be acknowledged and respected. But Jesus says to us as individuals that we must love our neighbour as ourself. So that whilst we may speak in a general way about those rights to food, care, education and the Gospel of Christ which each person has, it is proper that we should remind ourselves of the part which we as individuals must play in the honouring and respecting of those whom we meet in the course of our everyday life. For these people, however difficult and uncongenial some of them may be, are men and women made in God's image, and it is about these, the people amongst whom we live and work, that Jesus has said 'love your neighbour' – forgive him, understand him, be generous to him and about him, speak well of him, don't despise or dismiss him. See me and serve me, Jesus tells his disciples, in the people you meet, whomever they may be, and irrespective of how they treat you. For to despise, ignore, or scorn your neighbour is to fail to keep the sixth commandment; to treat your neighbour in an unloving, inconsiderate, unkind way is in a sense to kill him in your mind and heart.

The fifth commandment, 'Honour your father and your mother', speaks to the disciple of the respect which is due to his parents, who demonstrate to him the mercy, kindness and generosity of God our Father. The sixth commandment goes further and tells us that all people are to be given honour and respect. Indeed all are to be loved. For whilst the good parent speaks in a special, particular, way about the nature of God, all humanity mirrors that nature by virtue of the fact that we bear the divine image. For which reason the Christian disciplines himself, and prays for grace, that he may honour all to whom the gift of human life has been given. He cannot in any sense whatever kill the brother whose keeper he is in the sight of God. The commandment 'You shall not kill' is uncompromising and unqualified. So too is Jesus's restatement of it, 'Love your neighbour as yourself'.

7

'You shall not commit adultery'

This commandment concerns marriage. Like most of the other commandments it is framed in negative terms, but in saying what is wrong it simultaneously affirms what is right. Adultery – the physical union of two people who are not married to each other, and at least one of whom is married to someone else – is an offence against marriage. Indeed it is the betrayal of marriage, and in being this it serves to highlight what marriage essentially is as instituted by God. Many, perhaps the majority of people, are called to this state of life, which makes it necessary that any consideration of Christian living should give attention to it. Certainly the seventh commandment, with its injunction that no married person should betray his or her marriage-partner by committing adultery, leads us to examine the Christian understanding of marriage.

There would seem to be three distinctive features of this understanding. First, Christians see marriage as a vocation; they hold that some people are called by God to the state of marriage, just as some people are called to the single life, and just as God calls some people to the priesthood and to the life lived by a monk or nun. This is important, since this fact of vocation affirms the dignity of the married state straight away. There have been times in Christian history when marriage has been seen as a kind of second-best to celibacy, but this is wrong because no calling from God should be seen as inferior to another, and blessedness is to be achieved by fulfilling God's will for us, whatever that will may be. The falling in love by two people, and the consequent wish, after careful thought, to commit themselves to each other within the union of marriage – this we should see as something which has come about through the providence and goodness of God; a vocation given, heard, and answered. The giving of this vocation is a sign of God's love and care towards the two people concerned, and is a manifestation of his desire for their happiness and personal fulfilment. This vocation is a matter for joy and thanksgiving on the part of those who receive it, and because it is a vocation from God it is to be undertaken and pursued with faithfulness and determination.

Christian marriage is seen as a vocation; it is also a sacrament, one of those seven sacraments of the Church by which grace is bestowed upon us under some outward sign. In this sacrament of Holy Matrimony, the outward sign is the solemn promises which the two people make to each other, and the grace which is given is strength to assist them in the keeping of those promises. (We must always remember that grace is not something magical, which frees us from the responsibility to work for what is good; rather, grace is assistance from God which we must both receive and co-operate with.) It is a truth about the love and working of God that he never calls us to do anything without, at the same time, giving us the ability to carry it out. And so those who are called to marriage have available to them that grace which they need to enable them to fulfil their vocation. All relationships have times of stress and difficulty, and probably very few marriages are entirely free from times of strain. Marriage is certainly no easy option, and we see the wisdom and love of God in making marriage one of the areas in life where special grace is available by means of a sacrament.

Marriage is a vocation, a sacrament, and also it is a relationship which is distinctive insofar as it is a lifelong union. There is nothing temporary or provisional about Christian marriage; it is no mere convenient arrangement made for the time being. Echoing the words of Genesis, Jesus spoke of the two people who enter into a marriage as becoming, as it were, 'one flesh' (Matthew 19:5), and the physical union of man and woman which belongs within marriage is both a sign and an expression of the joining together of the two persons. It is this life-long nature of Christian marriage which gives it that valuable characteristic of stability: stability for the two persons themselves, because each knows where he or she stands in that their partner has made a solemn commitment; stability too for the children of the marriage, enabling them to grow up in the setting of their parents' life-long relationship.

You shall not commit adultery: adultery is the betrayal of that complete fidelity which the partners in a Christian marriage have solemnly promised to each other before God, and which is itself a reflection of that perfect fidelity which Christ the bridegroom has towards his Church, loving it, St Paul says, and giving up himself for it (Ephesians 5:25). For fidelity is an element which is fundamental to the Christian understanding of marriage, a relationship which is both life-long and exclusive, the two people giving themselves completely and fully the one to the other, with no taking back of their affection in order to bestow it upon another person. To some this ideal of life-long fidelity – the very antithesis of adultery – may seem to be an ideal which is hardly attainable, and perhaps not even desirable in a world where marital infidelity is so widespread and generally accepted. To this the Christian would reply that the ideal which the Church teaches is in fact attainable just because grace from God is available to those whose hearts are open to accept it, and who have a real desire and a real determination to live-out their marital commitment, both for his glory and for the ultimate benefit of themselves, their children, and their community. And further, that the ideal which God himself has set before us is what he, in his infinite wisdom and love, knows to be the thing which will make for the true peace and happiness of his people.

8

'You shall not steal'

All forms of stealing are condemned by the eighth commandment in the same way that all forms of killing are condemned by the sixth. In both cases there may be rare occasions when such a course represents the lesser of two evils; the defence of the innocent against oppression and violence may sometimes make killing permissible, and removal of what is harmful may similarly make stealing permissible in certain situations, but properly these things can never be other than the lesser of two evils. For the Christian they can never represent an absolute good. But whereas killing at least in its most literal sense is something clearcut and decisive, stealing is a sin which it is possible to drift into in a casual sort of way, hardly being fully conscious that it is in fact a wrong action which is suggesting itself. For whilst there are no minor killings and major killings, there are certainly petty thefts and more serious thefts; there is also perhaps something of a grey area between what is genuinely stealing and what is not. Furthermore, it is quite easy for us to persuade ourselves, or to be persuaded by others, that something which is in fact stealing 'doesn't really matter': 'The firm I work for doesn't really need these envelopes, or these pencils . . .'; 'It won't matter if I take some of these vegetables; there are so many of them and they won't be missed . . .'; 'It won't matter if I take this book away with me; it wouldn't really interest anyone else . . .' One of the favourite phrases of the devil as he seeks to persuade us to do what is wrong is 'It doesn't really matter', and he frequently tries to turn us aside from what is right by using it, not least when the matter concerned is honesty. 'Yes,' he says, 'of course it is wrong to steal, but taking, removing, borrowing this or that – well, does it really matter?' The devil never wishes us to call a spade a spade, and he is happy to supply us with euphemisms for stealing.

69

A further difficulty as regards right action in this area of our living, over and above the fact that we can easily be persuaded that stealing certain things 'doesn't really matter', is the fact that there are certain more subtle and less obvious types of stealing than the simple purloining of objects. We can, for example, steal the credit that is due to someone else for the doing of some good action. We can also steal another person's good name and reputation, and we can steal another person's friends, ideas, happiness or peace of mind. Also we can steal time – the time for which we are being paid to work and which, if we are not using it to our employer's advantage, is in fact being stolen from our employer. Essentially, stealing is taking away from another person that which rightly belongs to that person, and in taking from people what is theirs we are guilty of failing to respect those persons and so to love them as Jesus has commanded us. It is not too difficult to steal; on the whole it is easier than killing another person, and it is easy to persuade ourselves that it is either not a sin, or else one so insignificant that to refuse to commit it or to worry about it afterwards is to be guilty of over-scrupulosity and humbug. So the person who is seeking to live in accordance with the will of God has to exercise watchfulness and firmness, for the eighth commandment does not say 'It is wrong to steal valuable objects', or 'On some occasions stealing is wrong', or 'It is wrong to steal if you might be detected'. Rather it says in very definite and wholly unqualified terms 'You shall not steal'.

As we have seen, most of the commandments are phrased in the negative, but in stating what is wrong (through not being in accordance with God's will for us) they point us towards what is right. The commandment 'You shall not kill' reminds us of the wonder and value of human life; the commandment 'You shall not commit adultery' teaches both the nature and the sanctity of Christian marriage. In the same way the commandment 'You shall not steal' lays before us a positive good, and that is the characteristic of generous giving. For generous giving which is free from self-interest and condition

and which is marked by sacrifice and abundance, this is the
opposite of stealing, and it should characterise the Christian in
his or her daily living. In having this quality or characteristic
the Christian is very obviously seeking to follow Christ, both
in his teaching and in his living, and so to put on the likeness
of Christ who in all that he did and said displayed the divine
generosity. We might recall his generous self-offering made to
the Father on our behalf: we might consider the generosity
shown on the occasion when a vast amount of wine was made
(John 2:1–11); when an immense number of people were fed in
the wilderness (Luke 9:12–17); or when a huge catch of fishes
took place (Luke 5:4–7); or we might consider the generosity
shown to us in the frequency with which grace is made
available to us in forgiveness and in Holy Communion – grace
and life which are unlimited and all-sufficient. We might also
remember how Jesus in his teaching commended the generous
giving of the Good Samaritan (Luke 10:30–37); of the Owner of
the Vineyard (Matt. 20:1–16); or the Widow in the Temple
(Luke 21:1–4); and of the Father of the Prodigal Son (Luke 15:
11–32).

In accordance with the eighth commandment the Christian
is to be honest; he must not steal. But if he is to be a true
disciple of his master, he must be more than merely honest and
fair in his dealings with people. That is only a beginning. To
be Christlike is to give generously; to be generous in the giving
of time, talents, and money; to be generous in the giving of
patience, understanding, courtesy, and pardon. For generous
giving is a vital part of love; a characteristic of that love which
we receive by grace from God, and which we must lavish upon
one another.

9

'You shall not bear false witness against your neighbour'

Perhaps this commandment is less immediate and memorable than some of the others. Indeed we may have to pause for a moment in order to focus our minds upon what its subject actually is. But when we do so we realise that it concerns an important area of our dealings with our fellow-men and women, and hence of our Christian living. For this commandment concerns truthfulness, and it asserts the importance of truthfulness by condemning its contrary, lying. Furthermore it emphasises the wrongness of lying by citing a particularly unpleasant form of untruth – the bearing of false witness. To bear false witness is to testify that someone is guilty of some crime or misdemeanour when all the time the person bearing false witness knows the other to be innocent; this is a public kind of lying, and one which will most probably bear the consequence of the accused person being unjustly condemned and punished. There is something bare-faced, cruel, malicious, about the bearing of false witness which makes it perhaps the worst kind of lying, and the citing of it by the ninth commandment serves to throw the wrongness of lying into high relief. A readiness to deceive and to mislead is incompatible with Christian behaviour; openness and truthfulness are to characterise the disciple of Jesus.

But why? Why is it wrong to lie to and about people? What is it which makes this incompatible with Christian living? We know how easy it is to be untruthful, or at least not wholly truthful; we know too that untruthfulness can be very convenient on some occasions; we also know that the truth can hurt and is sometimes unacceptable. So why is the Christian charged with truthfulness and forbidden to lie? Perhaps the answer should be sought in the ways in which God has dealt with mankind. When we look forward to the coming of Christ in the season called Advent we sometimes sing a carol beginning 'This is the truth come from above' – words which echo Jesus's own saying 'I am the way, the truth, and the life' (John 14:6). Jesus is himself Truth; he came into the world to reveal God's Truth to us. He is the light which shines in the darkness, scattering the darkness of error, falsity, and ignorance. Opposed to the Christ and to his ministry of revealing the Truth to mankind is the devil, branded as the Deceiver (John 8:44): his 'ministry' is to deceive God's people – to convince them that there is no God, that life has no meaning or purpose, that nothing is required of us, that there are no standards worth maintaining and fighting for. By contrast, Jesus is the revealer of truth; he shows us the Father (John 14:9–10) and he makes known to us the eternal purpose which God has for us. He teaches us how to live and how to die, he tells us what things have lasting value, he gives us standards to live by and by which we can recognise truth, he teaches us how to achieve true and lasting happiness. The devil too offers us happiness, but in doing so he offers us a lie: he says that we will achieve happiness by luxury and ease, whilst Jesus teaches us that true blessedness comes through taking up the Cross and following him into pain and self-sacrifice. Jesus does not promise us ease in this life, but he does offer us the truth; unlike the devil, he never deceives us. He is indeed 'the truth from above'; he speaks to us in his words recorded in Holy Scripture and in his words spoken in the stillness of our hearts with that openness and truthfulness which belongs to love.

If, then, God's dealing with us is characterised by truthfulness, so that Jesus can apply the word 'Truth' to himself in an absolute way and properly be thought of as the one who brings light into our darkness and understanding into our perplexity, then surely just as God is truthful towards us, so we in turn must be truthful towards one another. It is inappropriate for those who are followers of Jesus, seeking to grow in his likeness, to deceive one another – that belongs rather to putting on the likeness of the Adversary, the arch-deceiver. We must, therefore, avoid the bearing of false witness, together with avoiding all forms of lying in our dealings with each other. In creation God has given mankind, every man and woman, a wonderful dignity, the dignity of being made in his image, and this is further enhanced by the fact that Jesus has shared in our humanity, not least for the purpose of revealing God's truth to us. For us to lie to people or about people is, in a way, to rob both them and us – the deceived and the deceiver – of a part of that God-given dignity. It is too a failure to treat our fellow-men and women with that respect which is due to them as having been made by God and loved by God. To lie to someone is nothing less than to abuse them; it is to treat them as if they were something less than what, by God's creative and redemptive work, they are.

All of us hate being told lies. We also hate lies being told about ourselves. It somehow make us feel abused and diminished. As human beings we have a right to the truth, and we in turn seek to love the truth and to avoid all pressures and temptations to indulge in lies. Only when all our behaviour is characterised by openness, honesty, truthfulness, will we be living in the likeness of Christ who is the true Light and who calls us in our turn to be lights shining in the darkness (Matt. 5:14–16).

10

'You shall not covet'

Covetousness, unlike stealing or killing or the committing of adultery, is an activity of the mind, and this brings before us that fact that Christian living not only concerns what is done, but also what is spoken and what is thought. The follower of Jesus seeks to regulate and bring under control all parts of his or her action, the verbal and mental no less than the physical. For discipleship concerns the whole of the person, and just as it is the whole person which Christ has redeemed and reclaimed, so the Christian seeks to give his or her whole person to the risen, living, and ever-present Christ. Further, the disciple is mindful of Jesus's teaching that to think, wish, or desire something is to be counted equivalent to having done it (Matthew 5:28).

What is the covetous person like? He or she is, at the heart of it, a dissatisfied person. He or she is dissatisfied with what they possess already, and looks at what another has got in an envious way. It may be another's possessions which are coveted, or it may be another's ability, success, or reputation. The fact that he or she has not got the object of their covetousness makes them resentful and maybe bitter or angry. It leads to the committing the sin of envy, and this has always been considered to be one of the deadly sins, capable of distorting and twisting the likeness of Christ in a person and powerful enough to destroy peace of mind and happiness. With this dissatisfaction the covetous person combines not only envy but ingratitude for what God in his love and mercy has given to that person; covetousness tends to drive out from the mind any enjoyment and appreciation of what is already possessed. Most likely the covetous person is also in the thrall of greed, an unattractive characteristic and one which is wholly inappropriate to the Christian, who is charged to have his or her mind fixed upon heaven and the attainment of those things which are eternal and of God (Colossians 3:2).

We see that covetousness pertains to disobedience to God, and as such is incompatible with Christian living in so far as covetousness involves a wrong kind of looking at one's fellow men and women. We have been commanded to love our neighbour, and loving our neighbour must involve rejoicing in the fact that God has given him or her good things – good gifts and good fortune. So it is appropriate as we look at our neighbour to give thanks for what he or she has been given, just as we give thanks for what we have been given; by contrast, it is inappropriate for us to look at our neighbour with feelings of resentment and envy. For love, St Paul says, is unselfish (I. Cor. 13:4), it is kind, and envies no one. Love is not concerned with acquisition – other than with the acquisition of the higher gifts – and it is certainly not concerned with that kind of acquisitiveness which stems from covetousness. To covet is to indulge in that selfishness which makes the loving of another impossible, for love is essentially a turning towards the other person and a consequent turning away from self and self-interest. Furthermore, a constituent of love is humility,and humility involves self-effacement and self-forgetfulness, and it precludes self-seeking. Whoever looks at others in a covetous way is not looking through the eyes of love; he or she is looking at them in a way which is incompatible with their profession as a Christian.

But those who covet are also looking at themselves, as well as at others, in a way which is flawed and ultimately improper. Or, in another sense, he or she is failing to look at themselves, failing to see the gifts which have been given to them and so failing to return thanks for those gifts. As a principle, Christians seek to look away from self; and yet there is a sense in which they should look at what God has made them and given them, just so that they may perceive the goodness, generosity and loving-kindness of God, and so be able to offer praise and thanksgiving. Insofar as the covetous person does look at himself or herself, they see only what they imagine themselves to lack – gifts which God has given to another but not to them. This attitude is negative; the person is disinterested in the gifts which he or she has, perhaps even oblivious to them. For Christians, the attitude of thanksgiving is fundamental to their outlook and to their response to God. They seek to practise the graciousness of looking at self in order to give thanks, and yet in this to be looking not at themselves but at God, who chooses to manifest his gifts in the lives of his faithful people, and who displays his wisdom both in the allocation or withholding of those gifts.

The ninth commandment 'You shall not bear false witness' points us to Jesus who is Truth. In the same way the tenth commandment points us to Jesus who exemplifies that generous self-giving and self-forgetfulness which is the very opposite of covetousness, with its wrong kind of self-regard and its desire to gain for itself what God has chosen to give to another. Writing to the Philippians St Paul said of Jesus 'His state was divine, yet Christ Jesus did not cling to his equality with God, but emptied himself to assume the condition of a slave, and became as men are; and being as all men are, he was humbler yet, even to accepting death on a cross' (Philippians 2:6–8). Christ is the pattern for the Christian, and in his self-emptying and self-giving we see an attitude which is utterly different from that which is marked by covetousness. For the person who is living in accordance with the pattern which Jesus has given us is concerned to give rather than to get, and within this Christlike attitude covetousness will never find a place.

Christian Prayer

CHRISTIAN PRAYER

(*The Lord's Prayer, from The Order for Holy Communion Rite A, in The Alternative Service Book 1980, copyright the Central Board of Finance of the Church of England*)

1

'Our Father in heaven . . .'

Our Father – these first two words of the Lord's Prayer point us to the heart of the Spiritual Life. They concern a particular relationship, the relationship between father and child, and this relationship is taken by Jesus as the model for that relationship which almighty God wishes there to be between himself and mankind. In choosing the words Our Father for the opening of the prayer which he gave to his disciples, Jesus is telling us that this is how we should think of God. And in doing so he is giving us an invitation, an invitation to trust, love, honour, depend upon God, for these are elements which characterise the right relationship between parent and child. Here then is a description of the relationship which God wants there to be between himself and mankind, an invitation to us to enter into that relationship, and also a declaration of God's love for his creature. Mankind, like everything else, only exists because God has chosen to bring it into being, and chooses to sustain it in being. And just as he chooses that we should exist, so it is for him to choose the nature of the relationship which there should be between himself and us. He reveals his love for mankind by choosing the relationship between father and child, an intensely personal and loving relationship, as the model for his relationship with us. Description, invitation, declaration – all these are contained in the model or image of Father with which Jesus begins his prayer. The spiritual life, or life of prayer, is about mankind's response to this invitation. It is about growing into the relationship into which God invites us, and thereby becoming ever more completely what we have begun to be by creation – namely sons and daughters of the King.

It is true that in one sense the parent/child relationship already exists between us and God insofar as we have been made by him and indeed made in his image. But in another sense, for a relationship to be authentic and to be truly personal it must have two active participants. Which means that the kind of relationship which God desires to have with us only comes into being when we for our part are both accepting and returning his love. God's love for us is perfect and complete —it has been so from eternity. But our love for him has to be enkindled and developed. Relationships are grown into, they are living, developing things, and this unique and wonderful relationship which the Spiritual Life is about is just such a living and developing relationship; it develops as our love for God, together with our personal knowing of God, increases. God made us just so that we might receive and return his love, and so it is in this relationship into which he invites us that our very purpose is fulfilled and accomplished.

But how do we come to know and love God, so that the parent-child model becomes a reality for us as individuals: in other words, how do we live out the spiritual life and attain our goal of unity with the One who both made us and who loves us infinitely? It is helpful to use a human analogy as a starting place. How do we come to know another human being, and come to develop a close personal relationship with them? Essentially, by spending time with them; by being attentive to them, by listening, watching, speaking, communicating; by being ready to break away from preoccupation with ourselves and concentrate upon the other person. In its simplest form this is how we come to know and love God, and the name which we give to this attentiveness to God is Prayer. Maybe the best, and certainly the most comprehensive way of describing prayer is simply 'being with God'J— being with him, that is, in a conscious way, for since he is present everywhere and always, we can never in truth be absent from him. 'Being with God' – this covers all the activities contained within prayer: speaking, listening, thinking, meditation, imagining, being silent with, together with all the traditional parts of prayer – thanksgiving, penitence, intercession, praise, adoration. Prayer is absolutely basic to the spiritual life because without communication there can be no personal relationship. Prayer is our willing response to the fact that God knows us and loves us, and wants us to know and love him. Without prayer the spiritual life cannot exist, and we cannot find our fulfilment and peace.

Yet if all this is to happen – if we are to enter fully into that relationship for which we were created – then two things must obtain in view of the fact of our human weakness and in view of the fact of the momentous thing which growth into God is. First, and on the part of God, there must be the bestowal of grace, the giving of that strength and enablement which is more than a mere injection of impersonal spiritual energy and resolution, and is more truly thought of as God's own self-giving – a communication to us of his very being. For we are changed and enriched not by something which remains essentially outside ourselves, but by what is bestowed upon us in such a way that it transforms us. Grace, which is a strengthening through God's self-giving, is bestowed upon us most especially in the Sacraments of the Church: in those Sacraments which are for all Christians – Holy Baptism, Confirmation, Holy Communion, and Penance – and in those which relate to particular situations and vocations – Holy Unction, Holy Matrimony, and Holy Orders. The Sacraments, because they represent the main channels of grace, have a very special place in the spiritual life. But the means by which God bestows grace are many and various, and notable amongst them are the various activities which are traditionally seen as forming part of the spiritual life, such as Prayer, Bible and other spiritual reading, Fasting and Almsgiving. The bestowal of grace, both through the Sacraments and by other means, is essential if our relationship with God is to be established and developed. This is God's reaching-out to us.

But, as we have seen, we must make response to that reaching-out: we must respond to God's invitation to enjoy that parent/child relationship which is suggested by the words

'Our Father'. So, second, there must be on our part the will, the desire, to grow in the knowledge and love of God – this is vital. And having that will, there must be the effort to be receptive to grace and to co-operate with it. Progress can only be made in the spiritual life if there is perseverance, and with it self-discipline. We must, if we are to grow in grace, and so grow in God, practise prayer, use the Sacraments, and utilise those other activities which form part of the spiritual life. By doing so we allow the work of the Holy Spirit in sanctifying us and drawing us into an ever-deeper and fuller union with God to proceed and flourish. God loves us, and we must play our part in the relationship which he proposes by loving him in return. To do so is to be true to our common vocation, and to come to possess fully the dignity and joy of being children of our heavenly Father.

2

'Hallowed be your name . . .'

In the first words of the Lord's Prayer Jesus gives us the model for our relationship with God, that of parent and child, and in doing so he sets before us the nature and the purpose of the spiritual life – that of establishing and deepening the very special relationship which exists potentially between ourselves and our Maker. Then in the second clause of the prayer, 'Hallowed by your name,' Jesus remind us that the fact that we are invited to enjoy this very close relationship with God must not lead us to approach God with any kind of casual familiarity. With our intimacy must go awe. God is indeed our Father, loving us deeply and tenderly. But he is also our Creator, our Lord, and our Judge. There are these two aspects to our relationship with God; we have to hold them in balance and reflect that balance in our life of prayer. Maybe, however, both attitudes come to the disciple fairly naturally. As a matter of experience, we know that we feel uncomfortable when we hear a fellow Christian speaking of God with that easy familiarity with which we might speak of an old friend just around the corner, and similarly we feel sad when another seems only to conceive of God as being some kind of remote and despotic headmaster. For most of us, the balance is, in practice, held by the rather differing ways in which we address God in the two basic parts of prayer – Public Prayer and Private Prayer. In the former kind, in liturgical prayer made with our fellow Christians, we traditionally use more formal language; we address God as 'Almighty and everlasting God', for example. Whilst in our private prayer, made on our own, we use more informal language, addressing God in the affectionate manner which is appropriate to a child speaking to its parent. Perhaps there is an analogy between this and the two kinds of language which might be used by the children of an earthly monarch in addressing their parent; one form of address is appropriate to the public occasion and another to the private.

Hallowed be your name: 'May you be given that honour, that reverence, which is yours by right'. Pre-eminently we play our part in the fulfilling of this petition by engaging in worship, for when we are worshipping as Jesus taught us to do, 'in spirit and in truth' (John 4:23), then in a very obvious way we are hallowing God's name. Furthermore, our worship also leads us in a particular way to fulfil the first of the two great commandments, that we should love God. For in the worshipping of God is the loving of God; indeed, it is at the very centre of our loving of God. In and by worship we are telling God that we love him, and expressing our love in a uniquely appropriate way. This is why worship can never be an optional extra for the Christian; it is basic to the spiritual life as a necessary part of the life of prayer, which is itself fundamental to his relationship with God. Further, the public prayer of the Church – the worship which it offers – has always been seen as the highest part of prayer. The prayer which we make as individuals matters greatly, and certainly our life of prayer is not complete without it, but individual Christians must remember that they are part of something greater than themselves, part of the whole body of Christ which, as a body, is called to offer its united sacrifice of prayer to God. First and foremost we are members of the whole rather than individuals, and so the prayer of the whole takes presedence. Further, it must also be remembered that the offering of worship is the chief task and function of the Church; there are other functions to be performed of course, not least the proclamation of Christ to the world, and yet worship, in which God's name is hallowed, remains the primary purpose of the Church, and centre from which all else proceeds.

Jesus taught us to make the petition Hallowed be your name; he also taught us that worship, by means of which God's name is hallowed, should be centred upon one particular activity. For there is only one act of worship which he expressly commanded his followers to perform: at the Last Supper which he ate with his disciples before his death and resurrection, he took bread and wine, gave thanks over them, broke the bread, and shared them with the disciples gathered around him in the Upper Room, using the words 'Do this in remembrance of me' (1 Cor. 11:24; see too Matt. 26:26–29, Mark 14:22–25; and Luke 22:17–19). In this way Jesus instituted the main act of Christian worship, and the Church, the people of God, has been obedient to this command since the time of the Apostles in every land and in every century. Sunday by Sunday the Christian family has met to celebrate the resurrection of Jesus by meeting around the Father's table, the Christian altar, to do what the Lord himself did and commanded his disciples to do as his memorial for ever. An ordinary family is never more clearly seen to be what it is than when it gathers around a common table for a family meal; just so the Christian family both is and is seen to be the people of God when it gathers around the altar. It is being true to its vocation as the Body of Christ as it meets in fellowship and in obedience to its Lord; it is meeting to offer the worship of the whole body and to experience the presence of the Christ who has died, who is risen, and whose return in glory it awaits. So it is that this particular act of worship, the Christian Eucharist, lies at the very heart of the life of the Christian church; it is the spiritual centre from which Christians go out to be Christ in the world, and to which they come back constantly to renew their faith and their strength.

But the Eucharist, Mass, Lord's Supper – the name is unimportant – the rite which lies at the heart of the life of the Church is much more than just a fellowship meal. Table fellowship there is, but the significance of what takes place is more profound. 'Do this,' Jesus said, 'as my memorial'. The Eucharist is the memorial of his saving work, of his dying and rising. The bread is broken and the wine is poured out – Christ has died. But present in that bread and in that cup after thanksgiving has been made over them, and the solemn words of Jesus 'This is my body', 'This is my blood', have been spoken, is the Body and Blood of the living and glorified Christ – Christ is risen. The dying and the rising are commemorated, the memorial which Jesus instituted is made. But this memorial is no mere recalling of events isolated in the distant past. For just as the Jewish people believed that by making an annual memorial of Passover-redemption caused them to actually enter into those saving events as a present reality, so the Christian believes that by making the memorial of Christ's dying and rising, those events became a present reality, and the disciple enters into the mysteries which are being celebrated. This memorial makes redemption present to us, and we are liberated by the saving death and resurrection of the Christ into whose presence we come. As we celebrate the Eucharist we are present at the Last Supper where it began, and we are present too at those joyful meals which Jesus ate with his disciples after his resurrection, at Emmaus (Luke 24:30–32), in the Upper Room (Luke 24:40–43), and by the lakeside (John 21:12–13).

Yet when we 'make the memorial' at the Eucharist, and enter into Jesus's saving work in a mysterious but actual way, we are indeed remembering, calling to mind; we are reminding ourselves of what Jesus has done to bring about our redemption; but even more important we are remembering before the Father Christ's redemptive action. We are holding before the Father the Christ who becomes present in bread and wine, and saying to the Father in effect 'Here is your beloved Son, who offered to you on earth and continues to offer to you at the altar in heaven his perfect sacrifice, made on our behalf. Look, Father, upon him and by the merits of his perfect sacrifice grant us your pardon and let us be reconciled to you.' Or, as a well-known hymn expresses it, the Church says to the Father as it makes the memorial which Jesus appointed:

> *Look, Father, look on his anointed face,*
> *And only look on us as found in him;*
> *Look not on our misusings of thy grace,*

Our prayer so languid, and our faith so dim;
For lo, between our sins and their reward
*We set the passion of thy Son our Lord.**

At the altar, then, as the Church makes the act of worship which is central to her life and being, the process by which we are redeemed is worked out and applied to us; we become recipients of Jesus's saving work as it both becomes present to us, and is set before the Father with the prayer that, as he accepts the offering which his Son has made, so he will accept us who by baptism have become members of the Body of Christ. We are liberated anew as we take part in the eucharistic action, and also we are given new strength to enable us to continue on our pilgrimage towards heaven and towards the completion there of our redemption For the Christ who comes to us in bread and wine is indeed the food for our journey and the means by which we are empowered to live and grow in him, and, as our relationship with him is central to the spiritual life – its very subject – so the means by which he comes close to us in his own appointed way must be of unique significance in our spiritual journey. Jesus said, 'I am the Bread of Life' (John 6:48), and it is at the altar that Christ the Bread of Life is received in the Sacrament of Holy Communion. It is for the Christian the principal channel of grace, and as such the joy and the centre of his or her daily living. Above all else it is in worship at the altar, at 'the Lord's own service', that God's name is hallowed, and that the Church is true to her vocation to offer God the sacrifice of praise and thanksgiving. Hence the celebration of the Eucharist should be considered as the characteristic, central, activity of the people of God, from which all else properly flows, and this is why Christians have met Sunday by Sunday from the time of the Apostles to do what the Lord himself did at the Last Supper and what he commanded us to do as his memorial.

* *New English Hymnal* 273

3

'Your kingdom come . . .'

Perhaps Kingship is the most ancient of all the images or models which mankind uses in his struggle to think and speak about God. It is widely used in the psalms, and despite the erosion, and indeed near disappearance of kingship as an institution in modern times, this model seems to be as popular as ever in contemporary religious choruses and songs. It is a rich image; it contains notions of power, splendour, order, protection, lawgiving, and judgement, and all of these notions can speak in one way or another about God and about the relationship which there is between God and man. But at the centre of this image of kingship is the notion of Authority; the authority which in this case belongs to God and which he exercises over all that he has made. Authority which extends in a particular way towards mankind in view of its ability through its characteristic of rationality, to accept, obey, and respond to that authority. In one sense the Kingdom of God automatically embraces all that is or can be since everything belongs to God as Creator. But in another and deeper sense the kingdom means those who actually choose to accept his king-ship, those who acknowledge his authority and make the decision to place themselves under it, recognising God's right to rule. We have this second sense in mind when we pray 'Your kingdom come'. When we say these words we are expressing the wish and the hope that all people without exception will open their minds and their hearts to God as King, joyfully and fervently seeking to obey his will and live as his loyal subjects.

Echoing this phrase of the Lord's Prayer, we sing in a familiar hymn:

> *Thy kingdom come, O God,*
> *Thy rule, O Christ, begin.**

Why? What is our motive for expressing this wish? Quite simply our love for God and, in accordance with his command, the love which we are seeking to have for our fellow human beings. Our love for God because it is his will – and, loving him, we wish his will to be obeyed – that the people with whom he has shared his attributes of rationality, of creativeness, and of the capacity for loving relationships, should enjoy the fulness of joy which he wants to bestow through his Holy Spirit. This fulness of joy and fulness of life can only come about, and so God's will be done, when a person lives in loving obedience to God's commands. In an unforgettable phrase St Augustine of Hippo expressed the belief that 'our hearts are restless till they rest in thee', and essential to this resting in God is the accepting of God's rule, his authority, his kingdom, and the consequent living-out of his commandments. Love of God, which involves the desire that his wise and perfect will should prevail is part of our motive for praying 'Your kingdom come'. The other part is love for our fellow men and women. Since they are to find their happiness, their fulfilment and their rest in living as members of the kingdom, and since true happiness is, consciously or unconsciously, the goal which every person is seeking, therefore our love for our fellow beings must involve our desire that they should enter into the kingdom by accepting Christ's rule. His commands are nothing else than a prescription for true and lasting happiness, and this, out of love, we wish all people to achieve. We recognise that his commands are not the fussy regulations of an officious and restrictive autocrat, but the wise directives of a loving father.

Then in another well-known hymn we sing 'The Church of God a kingdom is', and when we do so we remind ourselves that the Church which Christ founded and of which he is head is indeed the Kingdom of God. But as the Church already exists, and has done since Jesus sent the Holy Spirit to his disciples on the day of Pentecost, what exactly are we doing when we pray 'Your kingdom come'? Has it not come already? Yes, in one sense it has insofar as the kingdom has been inaugurated, but in another sense no, because two other things need to happen if the kingdom or rule of God is to be fully realised. First, we as individual members of the kingdom have still got to place ourselves fully under the rule of God. As yet there is much in our submission to the kingdom which is partial and imperfect. In all of us there remain areas of rebellion, blindness, and disobedience. We are not in the whole of our thinking, speaking, and action living as loyal and obedient subjects of our King. This means that both we as individuals and the Church as a whole must pray earnestly and penitentially 'Your kingdom come' – your kingdom come in me, your kingdom come in the Church which continues to be the wayward Bride of Christ. Second, we pray 'Your kingdom come' by way of petition that the wise and just rule of God may extend to all people; that everyone by placing him or herself under the lordship of Christ may find in him and in his kingdom the life and the truth, the meaning and the peace, which all are seeking to find in one way or another. The Christian prays without equivocation or uncertainty that all people everywhere may find the way, the truth, and the life in and through Christ and his kingdom, because Jesus did not say that he is a way, a truth, and a means of life, but The Way, The Truth, and The Life (John 14:6). Christians do not scorn or discount other religions, but cannot see them as containing that fullness of truth which is revealed uniquely in Christ. The Christian prays therefore that all people may find the door of the sheepfold, because, again, Jesus did not say that he was one door, but The Door (John 10:7), the Door by which all people are to enter into the joys of the kingdom. The Church, inaugurated by Jesus but yet to be realised in its fulness is like the seed which is growing (Matt. 13:31–32), or, to use another of Jesus's analogies for it, it is like the leaven in the lump of dough (Matt. 13:33). Our prayer 'Your kingdom come' asks that this process may continue and come to completion in due time.

Our prayer for the coming of the kingdom brings before us again the truth that in our relationship with God we are part of something infinitely larger than ourselves; we relate to him not solely or even primarily as individuals, but as part of the One Holy Catholic and Apostolic Church which is – however, imperfectly and in completely as yet – the Kingdom of God. The importance and significance of this fact is immense, for individualism, the mistaken idea that all that matters is our individual relationship with God, is a dangerous distortion of the truth. It is our common life in Christ, our membership of the whole body, the kingdom, which comes first. This does not at all mitigate against our individual value and indeed our individual responsibility; these stand firm. But the Christian should never feel or say that religion is essentially a private thing, something just between him or herself and God. The great images of the Christian life, such as soldier, competitor, or pilgrim, these all tell us of our common endeavour and vocation, for battles, competitions, and pilgrimages are communal things where a common purpose is shared and mutual support is given. The images used for the goal which we are seeking to win, the city of God, the feast in heaven, the heavenly choir – these, like the image of the kingdom are also common rather than private things. We have seen already how the common prayer of God's people, the worship of the Church, is primary, ranking before the private prayer of individuals, necessary though the latter is. Likewise it is our being members of the kingdom, subjects together of the one king, which is foremost – the first thing to be said about us as Christian people: we have undergone one baptism, we proclaim one faith, we are members of one kingdom, soldiers and servants of the one king.

Having thought about Christian belief and Christian living,

we are concerned in this part of the book with prayer, prayer as understood in its broadest sense so as to embrace the whole realm of Christian spirituality. The kingdom of God for whose coming we pray, the Church, this is the setting, the location, in which our spirituality is to be lived-out. It is within the fellowship of the Church, the Kingdom, that the Holy Spirit who indwells and animates Christ's mystical body sanctifies and inspires us. It is within the Church, and as members of the Church, that we are formed and sustained by the Sacraments. It is here, in this setting, that we offer God the worship in which our love for him is centred and expressed. It is as participants in the kingdom that our personal relationship with God, the knowing and loving of God, both grows and develops. 'The Church of God a kingdom is', and it is within this kingdom that life and salvation are to be found and possessed. A kingdom, of course, has confines; it has boundaries and laws, proper restrictions to be observed by its members, and so Christians control and regulate their actions in willing obedience to the teachings of the Christ whose kingship necessarily includes lawgiving. But all so that they may enjoy that fulness of life which God offers to those who acknowledge his kingship, and are received into his kingdom.

4

'Your will be done, on earth as in heaven . . .'

As we pray with hope and expectation for the coming of the Kingdom of God, so we look towards heaven as being the place where the kingdom is already realised, and which, as such, acts as a kind of model of what the kingdom will be like when it comes to completion on earth. In heaven, God's will is done fully and perfectly; the kingdom is accepted and lived-out by all. So that we who are living in that incomplete and imperfect part of the kingdom which exists here on earth can look towards the life of heaven to discover more about the character of the kingdom. And since living-out the kingdom centres upon that particular relationship with God for which we were made, we can see what it is that we are seeking to achieve by our practice of Christian spirituality.

'Your will be done, on earth as in heaven': by whom is God's will done completely and perfectly in heaven? Certainly by the saints in glory, whose excellence in this life was founded upon their aligning their wills with the will of God, wanting only what he wants, and entering more fully than most of their fellow-Christians into the mind of Christ. These, we believe, have already been admitted into the presence of God to behold his glory. But pre-eminently we think of God's will being carried out in heaven by the holy angels, those mysterious beings who for many people have been made incredible as a result of Victorian statuary and sentimental Christmas cards. Yet the being of the holy angels is attested through Holy Scripture, and nowhere more so than in the Gospels themselves. Their being certainly accords with scripture, and arguably with reason too. We are familiar in the natural world with beings which are wholly material, such as rocks, water, and vegetation. And we are also familiar with

97

beings which are partly material and partly spiritual – namely men and women who, having both body and soul might be said to have a foot in both camps. It seems, then, not unreasonable to suppose that there is another order of being, one which is wholly spiritual, and this we believe is angelic being. The angels are, in the correct meaning of the term, immaterial, and it belongs to their very nature to serve God constantly and perfectly, their wills totally aligned with his. They are, we usually say, 'unfallen'; their nature is not scarred by disobedience to their Creator in the way that human nature is scarred. They retain their original moral perfection, and without deviation fulfil the purpose for which they were brought into being. Quite simply, the angels do God's will.

But what more precisely is the function of the holy angels, what is their part in the divine economy? In what areas do we see their obedience to the kingdom? We probably think first and foremost of their performance of God's will not in heaven but upon earth. In the Gospels we are most familiar with their activity as messengers. Angels brought messages to Zechariah (Luke 1:11–20), to Mary (Luke 1:26–38), to Joseph (Matthew 1:20–21), and to the woman at the tomb (Matthew 28:1–7). But they also ministered to Jesus in the wilderness (Mark 1:12–13), and praised God (Luke 2:8–14). It is this latter function, in which we see them as it were turned towards God, that we are pointed towards the primary function the angels, that of offering God ceaseless adoration and praise, and it is this most essentially that we are speaking about when we consider the angelic perfection in doing God's will in heaven. In the Gospels, which concern God's gracious intervention in the sphere of our human action, we see the angels in their secondary role, that of messenger. But in the last book of the New Testament, the Revelation of John, the writer glimpses the court of heaven and there sees the angels fulfilling their other and most characteristic role. In St John's vision, the angels wait upon God, gazing, adoring, praising, glorifying (Rev. 5:11–12, 7:11–12). It is in this activity above all else that they do God's will, and fulfill the function for which they were created, that of offering worship to God.

But how is this digression concerning the nature and ministry of the holy angels relevant to our consideration of the spiritual life of the Christian? Simply because in fulfilling God's will in heaven by worship, praise, and adoration they point us again to our own vocation within creation, and to how we can most perfectly fulfil that will as we seek to play our part in its establishment upon earth. Men and women no less than the angels find their vocation, their highest ability, and their very meaning and purpose in the activity of loving God, which in turn finds its most natural and perfect expression in worship and prayer. For we share with the angels, and indeed with the whole of creation, animate and inanimate, the vocation of glorifying our Maker. The worship which the angels offer constantly in heaven is a model and an inspiration given to us. We, like them, are called to wait upon God, to be still and to know the wonder of his presence (Psalm 46:10). We too are called to place ourselves consciously, reverently, trustfully in his presence, and this we do when we pray. We recall that our final end, God's promise and our hope, is to enjoy the vision of God in heaven; to gaze for ever upon the one who is the unfailing source of all joy and peace, delight and contentment. As a hymn says:

> *What rapture will it be*
> *Prostrate before they throne to lie,*
> *And gaze and gaze on thee**

This looking upon God, this being still so that we may be filled with awe and wonder and love as we behold him, characterises the adoration which is offered by the angels in heaven, and it is something which we seek to nurture in ourselves as we strive to grow in the spiritual life. It will fit us for life to come,

---

* New English Hymnal 410

99

and it will enable us to live out our vocation more truly in this life.

Two rather practical things follow on from this as regards our practice of the spiritual life. In the first place, the Christian aims to grow in what is called Recollection, which is simply a loving awareness of the presence of God within and about us. For only as we grow in this will we be imitators of the holy angels in their constant worshipping of God. It is true that God is always present to us, it belongs to his very nature. But we are only truly present to him when we turn our hearts and minds towards him; when, in fact, we have that attentiveness to God which is of the very essence of prayer. Perhaps the radio provides an analogy; the radio waves are around us constantly, as God is. But we are only in touch with those waves, indeed, only aware of them, when we switch our radio on – when, by analogy, we turn to God and give him our attention. Our daily times of prayer, public or private, liturgical or informal, are certainly times when we are recollected; times when, like the angels, we are focussed upon God and giving him our loving regard. But for the rest of the time, or at least for much of it, God is absent from our thoughts as we go about our daily tasks and routines. Christians, seeking to do God's will as the angels do it in heaven, are aiming to live more and more of their lives in a state of consciousness of God's presence, or, as we say, in a state of recollection. The Christian aims to direct his or her attention to God more and more frequently in the course of the day, gradually advancing towards a state of constant recollection. There are various ways of promoting this in our life. In the Orthodox churches prominence is given to the so-called Jesus Prayer, 'Lord Jesus Christ, Son of the living God, have mercy upon me, a sinner', which the user repeats over and over again in time with his or her breathing so that in time it becomes part of the person's very being. Another way is to allow everyday sights and events to trigger-off short acts of prayer; for example, meals prompt acts of thanksgiving, the sight of hospitals and ambulances prompt prayer for the sick, churchyards prompt prayer for the departed. Dressing can suggest thoughts about putting-on Christ; undressing, thoughts of how we must one day put-off our mortal body; washing, of how we were cleaned in baptism; weeding, of how by grace we must pull-out and discard our faults and disobediences. Again, we can grow towards constant recollection in a maybe more formal way by letting there be regular, planned, moments of prayer during the day, in addition to whatever acts of worship we are able to take part in, and to our regular daily period of private prayer. Many Christians make an act of prayer at noon each day, using the traditional Angelus, which is a celebration of the Incarnation of Christ. Many, too, make a short act of prayer upon getting up in the morning and going to bed at night. And all, not least so that our awareness of God's presence, our recollection, is extended, spreading out into more and more of our time and thereby consecrating it. Perhaps it should be noted that being recollected is not the same thing as being so caught-up in the contemplation of God that we become oblivious to all else which, for people living ordinary lives, would bring life to a halt and herald catastrophe. No one, for example, would wish to undergo surgery at the hands of a surgeon who was practising this kind of recollection! No, the kind of recollection which we are seeking to grow in is a 'background awareness' of God's loving presence, and a consciousness of living within that presence. A prayerful attitude and approach to everyday living: one would certainly be happy about submitting to a surgeon who practised this.

The second thing which follows from the wish to imitate the holy angels in their doing of God's will in heaven is that, besides seeking to grow in recollection, the Christian also recognises the importance of the activity of silent contemplation within the life of prayer. It is true that the writer of The Revelation of John pictures the angels and saints in heaven as singing the praises of God, and certainly words have an important place in our prayer. Words are useful in expressing our thanksgiving, penitence, intercession, and praise. But we are surely not being misled when we tend to think of the company of heaven as being lost in wordless contemplation of God, lost 'in wonder, love, and praise', as they enjoy the supreme privilege of gazing upon the vision of God. Words have their limitation as well as their place, and it may well be that we use too many words when we pray. Words and images can be a barrier between us and God, and it is important to recognise that there are bounds to their usefulness. Peter on the mountain of the transfiguration was told to keep quiet (Luke 9:33–35); the right response at that moment was not the use of words, but the exercise of silent contemplation and adoration. In our life of prayer there are times when God likewise does not want our words but our loving and attentive regard. Two analogies may help us as we think about this kind of wordless prayer which we call contemplation. One is that of an elderly couple, happily married for many years living in perfect harmony with one another. They are content to sit together in complete unity of mind and heart, just happy to be together, and with no need to be constantly speaking to each other. As we come to know and love God better, we too become happiest when quietly enjoying his presence in a unity which is undisturbed by the use of many words. Another analogy is that of sunbathing. The sunbather lies on the beach soaking in the sun, enjoying its warmth without any need for words or action. Quiet prayer, contemplation, can be like this too. Simply a joyful relaxing in God's presence, soaking in his goodness and love.

We pray that God's will may be done upon earth as it is in heaven, and in this we are asking for grace to imitate the angels in their constant delight in God's presence; in their unceasing awareness of him and in their making of the offering of praise and contemplation. The aim of the spiritual life, we remember, is union with God, which comes from accepting and returning his love. It is in this that the Christian seeks to grow.

5

'Give us today our daily bread . . .'

When we ask God to give us daily bread we are recognising our dependence upon him, our dependence upon his mercy, love, and generosity for the continuance of our existence. And, as we ask, we are aware that it is not just the wellbeing of our bodies which is in his hands. We have a threefold nature, echoing the threefold nature of God, for we are mind and spirit as well as body, and each aspect of us needs to be sustained if it is to enjoy health and vigour. Most obviously the words 'Give us today our daily bread' refer to material food – food for the body. But Christian people have always understood this petition to relate equally to our need for spiritual food, food for the soul. Jesus spoke of this kind of food in his discourse recorded in the sixth chapter of St John's Gospel, and he makes this food available to his people in the Sacrament of Holy Communion. Food for the soul is just as necessary as food for the body, and Jesus said plainly 'Unless you eat the flesh of the Son of Man and drink his blood you can have no life in you. Whoever eats my flesh and drinks my blood possesses eternal life, and I will raise him up on the last day. My flesh is real food; my blood is real drink. Whoever eats my flesh and drinks my blood dwells continually in me and I dwell in him' (John 6:53–56). So for the Christian, seeking to deepen his relationship with God by leading the spiritual life, the Sacrament of Holy Communion is no optional extra. Rather it is an essential part of God's plan for the redemption and sanctification of his people, and a means by which that plan is realised. There is no kind of limit to the saving work of Jesus; it is whole people whom he is redeeming, people who are body, mind, and spirit. Our spirit, or soul, is fed at the altar by the Christ who gives his body and blood to be our sustenance, and the fact that this feeding can be pictured in such basic terms as

103

the provision of daily bread brings before us how essential this spiritual nourishment actually is. If we are to be what God intended us to be, and enables us to be, then we must receive grace. God in his wisdom has ordained that the chief means of grace available to us, the normal, the covenanted means of grace, should be the Sacrament of Holy Communion. It is life for the soul just as bread is life for the body.

But there is nothing impersonal or mechanical about this feeding of our souls – quite the reverse. They are fed by Christ coming to us and giving us his very self, his body and blood mysteriously present in bread and wine. So that the grace given in this sacrament is no mere injection of an impersonal spiritual strength, but is Christ the shepherd, the physician, the friend, the father, sharing with us his own risen life. The sacrament of the altar is no divine soup-kitchen, run on behalf of a distant and disinterested God: rather this is an encounter with the God who has died, who is risen, and who chooses in love to share his Easter victory with each of his disciples. The character of this healing and saving encounter can be seen in the circumstances of the institution of Holy Communion. Jesus gave us the Eucharist and the sacrament which lies at its heart in the intimate and poignant setting of a supper eaten with his friends. It was at that last supper, taken before he went out to face arrest, humiliation and death, that he gave his embryo church what was to be the chief means of grace through all the ages. He was about to be taken away from his friends. They would desert him in Gethsemane, and he would go forward alone to his trial, the pains of execution, the realms of death, and ultimately to the glory of heaven. Before being taken away, he provided a means by which he would remain present in a special and personal way to his people throughout their pilgrimage: present in the bread and wine which had been taken, blessed, broken and shared as his memorial.

But how can Christ, risen and glorified, be present in bread and wine, present in some special way over and above the way in which he is present everywhere by virtue of his

104

divinity? How can ordinary 'daily bread' become the means by which Jesus communicates to us his risen life; become, in fact, Christ himself? This the Christian accepts as being one of the great mysteries of the Faith, ultimately as inexplicable as how God is both Three and One, and as how Jesus combines in his one person both the divine and the human. These mysteries are beyond the comprehension of our limited understanding. There certainly have been times when the Church has attempted to 'explain' the presence of Christ in the sacrament of Holy Communion in philosophical terms, but in reality it is unhelpful to try to resolve the mysteries of God in such a way. Better the approach adopted in the rhyme attributed to Queen Elizabeth the first:

> *'Twas God the Word that spake it,*
> *He took the Bread and brake it,*
> *And what the Word did make it,*
> *That I believe, and take it.*

What happens when the Church does what the Lord did at the Last Supper, and sets bread and wine on the altar, making thanksgiving over them and speaking his words 'This is my body', 'This is my blood' is beyond our comprehension? Sufficient to believe that when Jesus spoke his words he was using no merely figurative language, for as we have seen, he said 'My flesh is real food; my blood is real drink' (John 6:55). Rather he was promising to be present with his people throughout time in a special and intimate way; present to be the 'daily bread' of the soul as it journeys through this life towards the banquet of heaven.

Two of Jesus's miracles point forwards in a very particular way towards the sacrament of Holy Communion which he would institute at the end of his earthly life, and these help us to understand this gift. They are the turning of water into wine at Cana (John 2:1–10), and the feeding of the large crowd of people with five loaves and two fishes (John 6:3–13). Both miracles speak most obviously of mystery, unfathomable and inexplicable, and both speak too of the care of Jesus to provide for the needs of his people: hungry people are fed in the countryside, thirsty revellers are satisfied at the marriage, just as countless generations of Christian disciples have been provided for at the altars of Christendom throughout successive ages. Here is the God who provides for his people as he provided for his ancient people on their journey through the wilderness, feeding then with bread from heaven (Exodus 16:11–31). In this, as in the two New Testament miracles, we see the God who supplies his people's needs abundantly; in the miracles, it is not a few bottles of wine which are provided, but a veritable flood of wine, maybe about one hundred and eighty gallons, and in the feeding of the five thousand it was not a snack which was provided but as much as the people could eat. The 'daily bread' given in Holy Communion is likewise abundant, enough to 'feed and train us up for heaven', as the hymn rather curiously puts it. *

Christians are lost in wonder and thanksgiving when they contemplate the gift given in the sacrament of Holy Communion. Here is the presence and the power of Christ, given in an extraordinary and very personal way. Here is covenanted grace, enabling the disciple to pursue his or her vocation. Here is an outpouring of the love of God, to which the Christian is invited to respond. And so the Christian approaches the altar with awe, reverence, penitence, and devotion. The Christian comes prayerfully to what lies at the centre of his or her spiritual life, to what is the well-spring of holiness and the channel by which Christ the living bread comes into his or her life and heart. Here Jesus binds us more closely to himself, making us his body in the world and his fellow-heirs in the kingdom of heaven.

* *New English Hymnal 274*

6

'Forgive us our sins . . .'

Union with God is the aim of the spiritual life; the opposite state to this union is separation and alienation from him, and it is brought about by sin. Sin is quite simply disobedience, mankind's disobedience to the revealed will of God. The classical expression of man's disobedience, of his turning aside from God, is found in the parable of Adam and Eve at the beginning of the Bible (Genesis 3:1–24). There, God directs that the fruit of a certain tree should not be eaten. Adam and Eve disobey, and by this act of disobedience their relationship with God is broken. They are separated and alienated from the source of life, freedom, and joy, and this is symbolised by their expulsion from the garden. For the Christian, sin is essentially disobedience to the two commandments given by Christ, the new Adam. When we fail either in the loving of God or in the living of our fellow human beings, then we fall into sin and our relationship with God is damaged as we enter into rebellion against him.

We see Jesus in the Gospels as the healer, healing damaged bodies and damaged minds. But the same Christ is also the healer of damaged relationships, and most particularly of that damaged relationship between mankind and God which sin brings about. By his saving work he had made it possible for this relationship to be restored and renewed. This comes about by the bestowal of God's forgiveness, and it can be given just because Jesus has offered himself to the Father as the perfect offering which brings about reconciliation, and thereby enables forgiveness to take place. By being forgiven by God we can be healed, cleansed, restored, and made free; we can even, as St Paul puts it, be 'made righteous' (Romans 5:19). And so it is possible for us to ask that our sins be forgiven.

But what is our part in this process of being forgiven?

What must the Christian do to enable the bringing about of that restoration which forgiveness effects? Since such forgiveness is necessary for the unimpaired relationship with God which is the aim and object of the spiritual life, this is clearly an important area in the whole field of spirituality. Our part in the process is to practise penitence, and penitence is *being* sorry for the sins that we have committed. Being sorry, it should be emphasised, not feeling sorry: penitence is not to do with the feelings, over which, ultimately, we have little control, but with the will – with decision and subsequent actions. What is involved in being penitent, what must we do in order to have that disposition which leads to forgiveness? There are three parts to being penitent. First there must be the recognition that we have disobeyed God, thereby damaging our relationship with him: we must take the trouble to ask ourselves just how it is that we have failed him through failing to keep the two great commandments. In what thoughts, words, and deeds have I disobeyed God by being unloving, unkind, impatient, ungenerous, thoughtless, hurtful, and mean? And besides the wrong things which I have done, what good things have I failed to do? I have failed God in failing to love my neighbour, and I have also failed God in not loving him as I should do, through my life of prayer and worship. We find that we have fallen short of the standards which God has set us and which we have set ourselves. Recognising our sin, facing up to it, is the first part of penitence; we have to confess to ourselves before we can confess to God, and this involves being completely honest and realistic with ourselves. We can hardly expect God to forgive us our sins if we do not take the trouble to recognise what they are; hence self-examination is the starting place. Then, second, we must genuinely wish to receive forgiveness from God, and a test of this – as well as an important part of penitence in its own right – is our firm intention, made as an act of will, that we will do our best (with the help of grace) to avoid those sins which we have committed in future. Penitence has a backwards reference – the recognising and deploring of our past faults; it also has a forwards reference insofar as our intention for the future is involved. Penitence is neither complete nor genuine unless it involves what is usually called a 'purpose of amendment'. The third part of penitence is the confession of our sins; the formal owning-up to God that we have disobeyed him. Of course God knows already, and better than we do, how we have failed him. Just as the parent probably knows full well that the child has broken the window or left the hen-house door open. But the actual admission has moral value as the action by which we take responsibility for the sin. The admission or confession is therefore a necessary part of the process of penitence; it is a kind of placing ourselves before God, humbly and sorrowfully, just so that we may be forgiven.

But how and when do we come before God to confess, to own-up to our faults? Just as there are three basic parts to penitence so there are three different ways or contexts in which confession can be made. First, we can quite simple tell God our faults in our private prayer, and if we do so honestly, thoroughly, and with purpose of amendment, then our hearts will certainly be open to receive his forgiveness. Second, we can join in the 'general confession' which usually forms part of the eucharistic rite. It is assumed that we will have examined our conscience beforehand and have thereby prepared ourselves to join in what, liturgically, can only be a general kind of confession. When we confess our faults in this way, we receive from the priest who is presiding at the Eucharist a 'general absolution' in words such as 'Almighty God have mercy upon you, pardon and deliver you from all your sins'. In doing this the priest is exercising one of the distinctively priestly functions, that of pronouncing God's forgiveness. After his resurrection, Jesus said to his apostles 'Receive the Holy Spirit. If you forgive any man's sins, they stand forgiven; if you pronounce them unforgiven they remain.' (John 20:23). Christians believe that this ministry which Jesus entrusted to the apostles was not intended for the apostolic age alone, but rather to be passed on within the continuing ministry of the Church. Authority to pronounce the forgiveness of sins is therefore passed on to the priest at ordination, and is exercised as part of the function of priesthood. It does not of course mean that priests forgive sins on their own account; rather, they act in the name of God and as an instrument of God. Always it is Jesus who says 'your sins are forgiven', just as it is Jesus who says at the altar 'This is my body, this is my blood'.

The third way of confessing our faults and of receiving God's forgiveness is by making a confession of sin privately in the presence of a priest. Many Christians see this as one of the seven Sacraments of the church; it is called The Sacrament of Penance of The Sacrament of Reconciliation, but is often referred to simply as Confession. In essence it is the same as the second way outlined above, except that the general confession and absolution, made and received in company with others, is replaced by a particular confession of sins, made in the hearing of the priest, together with a particular absolution (or pronounce-ment of forgiveness) given by the priest. Not least amongst the advantages of this third way is that it involves the Christian in actually getting down to self-examination, which, without this discipline, can easily be neglected with a consequent failure to know both what needs forgiving and what is to be avoided in the future. Another advantage is that the priest in whose presence the confession is made has the opportunity to give 'counsel' – advice on how to attempt to overcome the faults confessed, together with words of encouragement and comfort. The priest has a further role in being a representative of the Christian body as well as being a representative of God, and this pertains to the fact that by our faults and failings we sin against the Christian community as well as against God, insofar as the Church, the whole body, is weakened, however slightly, by every sin committed by one of its members. Hence it is right to confess to the Church, represented by the priest, as well as to God. Finally, it can be very therapeutic for the person making the confession – the penitent as he or she is usually called – to actually unburden his or her conscience in this way, in a setting where he or she can find acceptance and support together with the reassuring pronouncement of God's forgiveness. Those who seek forgiveness in this particular way testify to the feeling of liberation which comes from this life-giving encounter with the Christ who died and rose so that the burden of sin might be lifted from us, and that we might make a new beginning by his grace. For many this encounter is a deeply moving experience of the love of God.

These, then, are the three customary ways by which a Christian makes confession of sin: in private prayer, in a public general confession, or in private with the assistance of a priest. Three ways of seeking God's forgiveness, and ways in which are not exclusive options; may Christians practise all three at different times. We may well confess our faults in our private prayers at the end of the day, or in our preparation for receiving Holy Communion; then join in the general confession at the Eucharist; and then use the Sacrament of Reconciliation perhaps three or four times a year. The vital and necessary thing, of course, is that the Christian does by one means or another actually get down to the practice of penitence, giving due regard to this particular part of prayer. For without penitence and the forgiveness which answers it the channels of grace between God and our soul remain blocked, and our spiritual life and growth will be impaired.

7

'As we forgive those who sin against us . . .'

An essential part of the Christian character is a forgiving spirit, a capacity and a readiness to forgive those who have in some way wronged or harmed us. This matter may seem to pertain to Christian living rather than to the life of prayer, and so be out of place in this part of our consideration of the Christian way. But since the life of prayer, or spiritually, concerns the whole of our relationship with God, the matter of a forgiving spirit is entirely relevant, because that relationship depends on our being obedient to God in all our attitudes. Our life of prayer and our essential character are inseparable. Only if our will is aligned with God's will, and only insofar as we are seeking to put on Christ and become Christlike, will our prayer be real and our relationship with God be authentic. 'As we forgive those who sin against us' is the only phrase in the Lord's Prayer in which we say anything about our own attitudes and consequent actions; it brings before us the fact that these must be brought into line with God's will if our prayer is to be sincere and acceptable to God. For our relationship with him depends upon the presence of trust and obedience in us; a readiness on our part to do what God wants us to do however difficult, demanding, and unconducive that may be.

It is God's will that we should forgive our brother. This is made clear in the phrase 'As we forgive those who sin against us' which follows on from the petition that we ourselves may be forgiven. The juxtaposition of the two phrases is significant. We are led into a kind of understanding or agreement with God. He will forgive us our offences if we in turn will forgive others. It is more than reminding ourselves that it is appropriate for us to forgive if we wish to receive forgiveness, something which is desirable and commendable. Rather it is a pledging or

112

undertaking on our part, the entering into a kind of bargain. And a recognition too that if we are not prepared to forgive, then there can be no assurance that God will forgive us. If we are not prepared to forgive, then we must be prepared to remain unreconciled ourselves, cut off from God by the sins which we have committed. Much is at stake; a forgiving spirit is no desirable but dispensible appendage for the Christian – rather his or her spiritual life and health depend upon it.

But Jesus does more than present this 'agreement' to the Christian in the prayer which he gave to his disciples. The importance of forgiving others is a recurrent theme in his teaching. The unlimited quality of the Christian's readiness to forgive is stressed in the answer which Jesus gave to Peter's question 'Lord, how often am I to forgive my brother if he goes on wronging me? As many as seven times?' to which Jesus replied 'I do not say seven times; I say seventy times seven'. In recording this saying St Matthew illustrates it by the parable of the king settling his accounts, in which the servant who refused to forgive his fellow-servant a small debt, when he himself had been forgiven a large debt, is held up for condemnation. Echoing the words of the dominical prayer, Jesus ends the parable with the words 'and that is how my heavenly Father will deal with you, unless you each forgive your brother from your heart' (Matthew 18:21–35). Then in another parable, that of the Prodigal Son, Jesus clearly commends the father who has been wronged by his younger son, but who is ready to offer him forgiveness; the action of the father is not merely commended, but is given as a picture of God himself in his dealings with mankind. In his readiness to forgive us, he gives us a pattern for how we must react when we have been wronged (Luke 15:11–32). As always, Jesus in his own actions and attitudes perfectly exemplifies his teaching – his life is always the perfect illustration of his words. And so in the course of his passion, when he was most terribly and cruelly wronged, he was ready to forgive his tormentors and persecutors – 'Father, forgive them for they know not what they do'

(Luke 23:34). It is clear that the Christian must, as part of his or her putting-on of Christ, acquire that forgiving spirit which Christ both taught and exemplified. To refuse to forgive someone is consequently nothing more nor less than to refuse the clear command of Jesus, and therefore to be in rebellion against him.

But of course the Christian does not pretend that to forgive is easy, still less that doing so comes naturally; the wish for vengeance is a common element in our fallen nature. As with penitence, however, the process of forgiving belongs largely to the will, over which we have control, rather than to the feelings, over which we have relatively little control. When Jesus commands us to forgive our neighbour he is not asking us to screw up some warm — or at least tepid — feelings towards the person who has offended us. Rather we are being asked to enter into a process which has three parts, and which is concerned with the exercise of the will. First, we must make the decision that we wish to forgive the person concerned, a wish that will be based upon our eagerness to obey Jesus's command, and to follow the example which he has given us; the wish quite simply to align our will with his will. Having chosen through obedience and love to forgive rather than to harbour resentment and ill-feeling, the next step is to ask God for grace, for divine help, in making the decision operative. We are only too aware of the limitation of our own resources of charity, and in this situation it will be necessary to rely upon the grace which has been promised to us when we ask in faith (Luke 11:9). Only with this help will our attitude towards the person who has offended us be changed, so that we come to see that person as God sees him or her rather than through the eyes of human resentment. This is not asking for 'warm feelings', but for genuine charity; for infused love rather than any kind of self-generated affection. Then third, having made an act of will, a decision based on obedience, and having sought grace to effect it, we must co-operate with grace by making an effort to treat the person concerned in a way that is compatible

114

with having forgiven him or her. We must be careful to speak to the person and about him or her, act towards the person and even think about him or her, in a way in which we would do if the offence had never been committed. This is a necessary part of reconciliation – the restoring of the person to the place which he or she had before they caused us harm. God in forgiving us has given back to us the status of sons and daughters – it has become as if we had never offended, our sin is remitted. We likewise are to allow just such a restoration to be effected in our relationship with our enemies; the offence is to be washed away. If we see the exercise of forgiveness in these terms, as concerned with obedience, an exercise of will, and the bestowal of enabling grace, then the Christian can never truthfully say 'I cannot forgive', however, much he or she is sinned against. 'I cannot forgive' is more correctly interpreted as 'I will not forgive, and this is an attitude which is quite unacceptable in the disciple; it is a preferring of one's own will to that of God and consequently a failure to accept the kingdom.

Jesus says 'Love your enemies' (Matthew 5:44), and the forgiving of those who sin against us is one of the most obvious ways whereby this love is exercised. Furthermore, a forgiving spirit is not only one of the very attractive features of the Christian character but one which is most obviously a Christ-like characteristic. It has within it something of that humility, that patience, and that gentleness which belong to the love which the disciple is called to practise. Furthermore it marks the Christian as living in accordance with another order, living, one might say, on the supernatural rather than the natural plane, and following the ways of the kingdom rather than the ways of fallen human nature. So Christians seek to grow in a forgiving spirit, and pray that it may be given to them. It follows from their desire to be united with the Christ in will and in deed.

8

'Lead us not into temptation . . .'

As we have already seen, one of the gifts which God has given us, and which distinguishes us as human beings, is the gift of free will. We have the ability to make choices, and thereby come to reasoned decisions concerning our behaviour. This is clearly a precious gift, and yet at times God's giving of it seems almost irresponsible in view of the foolish and even wicked choices which people can and do make. But the alternative, mankind without free will and unable to make any free choice, would mean that men and women were reduced to being mere robots. We would certainly be unable to choose anything which is opposed to the wise and good willing of God, but we would also be unable to choose freely anything which is good, noble, or generous. We would be unable to choose to ally our will with the will of God, and by this we would become devoid of all moral worth and value. Our goodness would have no more moral value than the greenness of grass or the wetness of water, and we would be unable to glorify God by choosing out of love for him what is right and good.

Mankind's freedom of will, and so of choice, is the background to our experience of temptation, because temptation is the suggestion made to us that we should choose what we know to be against the will of God, and hence to be morally wrong. Temptation is having before us two alternatives, one of which we must choose, and knowing in our heart that one of the courses of action represents conformity to God's will, whilst the other is contrary to his will. Further, it is an essential element in temptation that the wrong course is always attractive; necessarily so, because no one is inclined to choose what is manifestly unpleasant and undesirable. It is attractive, that is, to some source of weakness which we have – perhaps to our pride, or to our physical appetites. Eve, in the prototype

116

temptation situation described in the early chapters of the book Genesis, 'saw that the fruits of the tree was good to eat, and that it was pleasing to the eye and tempting to contemplate' (Genesis 3:6); she knew that the option of eating the fruit was not in conformity with God's revealed will, but the option was appealing. Often, however, when the Christian is tempted the wrong choice is not only more superficially attractive, but the moral issue itself becomes blurred; as part of the temptation, the idea that the right is genuinely right and the wrong actually wrong is challenged. Indeed, the one may be presented as the other, and the person being tempted may be persuaded that what he or she knows deep down to be wrong is actually right. The temptation may also be packaged in a whole range of allegedly extenuating circumstances, and be accompanied by all kinds of specious excuses for accepting the course to which one is being tempted. Fundamentally, however, temptation is suggestion: suggestion that we should choose to do, say, think, or possess something which we find attractive, but know in our heart to be inconsistent with the loving of God and of our fellow men.

What is the source of such suggestion? Where does temptation originate? Traditionally the Christian would speak of the Adversary, the devil, as the fountainhead of temptation – the same tempter who fulfils that role in the Adam and Eve story. Indeed, the activity of temptation has always been seen as the primary activity of the devil, and as the chief means by which he attempts to fulfil his purpose of disrupting God's work through distracting, disturbing, and discouraging God's people. Christians have always seen the devil as being set upon disrupting the divine plan of redemption, a work he seeks to perform by persuading people to turn away from God through disobedience. Today, of course, there are many who would be unhappy about positing any kind of personal power of evil, and who would not choose to speak about a devil who seeks to promote disobedience to the will of God. Such people would prefer to see the suggestion of wrongdoing which we call temptation as arising from the darker and less controlled aspects of the character and of society, with that attractiveness which the wrong course is seen to have as being sufficient in itself to lure the victim into adopting it. They may be right, but there is always the fear that we may be playing into the Adversary's hands by denying his objective being!

The Tempter is certainly seen in a personal and objective way by the Gospel writers Matthew and Luke when they describe the temptation of Jesus in the wilderness (Matthew 4:1–11, Luke 4:1–13). In these accounts the Adversary lays seemingly attractive suggestions before Jesus, which he immediately recognises as temptations to sin and consequently rejects. These two things, recognition and rejection, are vital in the Christian's response to temptation. Often, as we have seen, the temptation presents itself (or is presented by the Adversary) with a blurring of issues and maybe a further suggestion that the course of action in question is only negligibly wrong, or perhaps even positively good. The Christian has to cultivate a clear and ready discernment of what is right and wrong, which involves the development of a sensitive and informed conscience. Such a conscience may develop from a careful study of the moral teaching of the Church, or maybe more simply through serious reflection upon the implications of Jesus's two commandments, of how they are to be applied in the complex situations in which the Christian finds him or herself in the course of everyday life.

Year by year the Church meditates upon the temptations of Jesus in the wilderness at the beginning of Lent, the forty-day season of the Christian year in which God's people prepare themselves for the celebration of Christ's saving work, his dying and his rising, during Holy Week and Easter. One of the themes and aims of this season is the acquisition of a deeper love of God, and this necessarily involves the recognition and rejection of temptation because if we fall into sin then we become estranged from God rather than more closely united with him. How, as we consider the temptations of Jesus as this point in the Christian year do we week to fortify ourselves against the temptations which come to us? Chiefly by the practice of three disciplines which are particularly associated with Lent, although not by any means confined to it. These disciplines are Fasting, Almsgiving, and Prayer.

Fasting is a discipline which is commended to us by Jesus's own forty-day fast, and Christians all down the ages have found it to be a spiritual discipline which is effective in strengthening the will to resist temptation. How is this? Because essentially fasting provides a training-ground in which we can get practice in saying no to our inclinations. In Lent – or outside Lent – a person may choose to abstain from some particular food, meal, luxury, or activity which they enjoy (fasting being a term which can be given a wide reference, and which does not necessarily imply total or partial abstinence from food). This voluntary abstaining from things which are not in themselves wrong provides the Christian with practice in refusing what is attractive and desirable, just so that when temptation actually presents itself the will is experienced and strengthened in refusing. But besides providing practice in exercising self-control, fasting also seems to be effective in heightening spiritual awareness and perception, in the same way that self-indulgence seems somehow to dull and blunt that awareness and perception. Fasting seems to make the Christian more aware of the divine presence and of his or her own vocation as a soldier and servant of Christ. Almsgiving, the second discipline associated with Lent, acts in the same kind of way: self-denial is involved together with a recognition of the needs of others, and this assists the Christian in looking away from him or herself and in escaping that self-interest and self-indulgence which weakens the ability to resist temptation.

Prayer is the third of those three disciplines which assist in the recognition and rejection of temptation, and which are given special emphasis in the season of Lent. It has a vital role to play; like almsgiving, it helps us to turn away from self-interest, and like fasting it heightens our spiritual perception and discernment. It is in itself the turning of the soul towards God, and we see how Jesus in the wilderness turned towards the Father in answering the Adversary's temptations: 'Scripture says "Man cannot live on bread alone; he lives on every word that God utters"' (Matthew 4:4); 'Scripture says, again, "You are not to put the Lord your God to the test"' (Matthew 4:7); 'Scripture against says, "You shall do homage to the Lord your God and worship him alone"' (Matthew 4:10). It is noteworthy that Jesus was tempted at the very time when he had gone into the desert to pray, to spend time in spiritual communion with the Father before beginning his public ministry. Christian experience tells us that it is just when we are seeking to draw closer to God by prayer that temptation to wrong action, thought, and speech most often asserts itself. It is almost as if the Adversary is angered by our desire to grow in grace, and is determined to disrupt the movement of the heart and soul in a Godward direction. Certainly, the onset of temptation is one of the hazards of the spiritual life, and the battle against it, fought in union with the Christ who was himself tempted, is a conflict in which every Christian must become engaged.

9

'But deliver us from evil . . .'

Evil, like love and prayer, is a word which has a wide reference. First, it covers the whole area of sin, moral evil, which is essentially mankind's disobedience to God; men and women's acceptance of that suggestion which we call temptation, and their consequent breaking of one or other of the two great commandments of Jesus that we should love God and love one another. Of those things which make up the totality of evil, perhaps moral evil is the most clear-cut. A further area of evil is what is sometimes called natural evil: famine, disease, natural disaster. Things which bring pain and misery which seem to be both pointless and quite independent of human sin. This is a kind of evil which seems almost to be built into creation, and which causes immense suffering and sorrow to completely innocent people. And then a third and much less easily defined area of evil would be that of spiritual evil, the evil power which in Christian thought has been particularly associated with the Adversary; a power at work in the universe which is in deadly opposition to the love and the work of God, and which it is determined to disrupt and destroy. This form of evil, as we have seen, is denied objective reality by many; it is considered by them to belong to a benighted and superstitious way of thinking which has now been exposed and superseded. This of course must be a matter of opinion, but belief in such an objective power of evil is certainly too firmly rooted in Christian thinking to be lightly dismissed.

Together, these three areas produce what is often referred to not just as the fact of evil, but as the problem of evil. How can a God who is all-good and all-powerful, it is argued, permit there to be evil in his creation? Can it be, some suggest, that God is perhaps not entirely good, or else not entirely powerful? The Christian, who would maintain that God is both almighty

121

and the very source of good, is challenged to give an answer. He might begin by pointing out that moral evil, sin, is simply a consequence of mankind having been given free-will. Without freedom of will, men and women would have no moral worth; freedom of will is good, but there is a price to pay. That price is that mankind can misuse that freedom, and through deliberately making choices which are opposed to the will of God, can commit sin. Hence moral evil is not of God's making; it comes about through men and women's disobedience. Spiritual evil, too, can be seen as the result of disobedience indeed of rebellion. In traditional Christian thinking the Adversary and his associates have been thought of as angels in revolt, spiritual beings who have set themselves up to oppose that essential goodness of creation which comes from its divine authorship. Both moral and spiritual evil, therefore, can be understood as being consequential upon that freedom of will, and hence of choice, with which God has endowed both human and angelic being. Perhaps it is natural evil – disease, famine, natural disaster – which is the most difficult area to come to terms with, and which poses the most serious question for the Christian. Why should a child die of cancer? Why should thousands of people be dying of starvation, or hundreds be killed through a terrible flood? Where, in these cases, is that God who loves what he has made? 'Has God forgotten to be gracious?' (Psalm 77:9). Some may choose to speak of the natural order as being somehow infected by mankind's disobedience to God, but in truth there are no easy, ready, or convincing answers to this part of the problem of evil; it remains an area of mystery. There are, perhaps, certain insights into it: the experience of suffering can in some circumstances ennoble the character; it can enhance the individual's sensitivity to others, and call forth love and understanding. But if these are indeed insights, they are certainly no more than that. At the end of the day the Christian has simply to trust God. However, the fact that we have no answers to the problem is quite different from asserting that there are no answers; our understanding is finite, and we are not forced to the conclusion that by permitting evil to be rooted in creation God is showing himself to be less than all-powerful and less than good. We are simply confessing that it is beyond our limited understanding. The non-Christian may well argue from the fact of evil to some weakness in God; the Christian would argue in the other direction, starting from an assertion of God's power and goodness, and saying that this implies that evil must at least be capable of being turned to good account in the totality of God's plan. The Christian would also draw attention to the fact that Jesus, God the son, has entered into our human suffering (Phil. 2:8); he would adduce this not as being either an explanation nor as a palliative of human suffering, but as giving a new context in which the experience of suffering is to be understood.

The Christian prays for deliverance from evil. For deliverance, we should note, and not for immunity or total avoidance. For all of us become involved with evil in one way or another, not least through our own disobedience to God's will. In praying for deliverance we are essentially asking that evil may not cut us off from God; that it will not impede or destroy that union with God which is the aim of the spiritual life. For to be cut off from God is to experience what the Christian calls Hell, separation from the One who is the source of all peace and joy being the chief characteristic of hell. As we have already seen, sin, disobedience, cuts us off from God. So, too, can that kind of rejection of God which results from a failure to trust him when confronted by the fact of natural evil. And so, too, does surrender to those evil powers which seek to deceive us, blinding us to the truth, beauty, and goodness of God. From all of this, from moral and spiritual evil, and from the false inferences which can be drawn from the existence of natural evil, we seek deliverance. Such deliverance comes of course through the grace of God, and this grace is ministered to us most especially in the Sacraments which God has given to his church. We have already considered the two primary Sacraments, Holy Baptism and Holy Communion, which by the bestowal of Christ's risen life have a unique and central place in the deliverance of the disciple from the power of evil. But we must also consider in this context those two sacraments which have not yet been mentioned, Confirmation and Holy Unction, since both of these in their different ways are concerned with deliverance from evil.

Confirmation is part of the process of Christian initiation; it belongs as such with Baptism and with the first reception of Holy Communion, and in the early centuries it was normally administered in conjunction with them. The outward and visible part of this sacrament is the laying-on of hands with prayer by a bishop, or sometimes by a priest having a special commission from a bishop to carry out this ministry. There has been debate concerning the precise nature of the spiritual gift bestowed, but it is generally agreed that a strengthening of the recipient to lead the Christian life is given; a strengthening by and through the Holy Spirit, and one which answers the determination of the disciple to live in accordance with his or her baptismal promises, rejecting the powers of evil and turning towards God with faith and love. This strengthening through a special bestowal of grace is to be seen as part of the deliverance which is made available to us all; deliverance comes from God, and it is operative here in the enhanced ability which grace gives the Christian to resist temptation to sin, to remain faithful to God through the onslaughts of doubt which may be occasioned by natural evil, and to avoid falling away in the face of attack by the Adversary.

If Confirmation facilitates deliverance by means of a general, overall strengthening of the Christian, the Sacrament of Holy Unction gives such assistance in a very particular situation, namely that of serious illness. Holy Unction is the anointing of the sick as commended in the Letter of St James (3:14–15), and the outward and visible part of this sacrament is olive oil, blessed for the purpose by a bishop and applied to the sick person by a priest. Using the oil, the priest makes the sign of a Cross (the emblem of Christ's victory over the powers of evil) on the sick person's forehead, and sometimes on his or her hands and breast as well. The spiritual gift which is given is healing, healing in its widest sense. It may, if it is God's will, be healing of the body, and the words of St James, together with those of Jesus when he sent out his disciples with the direction that they should anoint the sick (Mark 6:13), certainly seem to encourage that expectation. If, however, God chooses in the individual case not to give physical healing through this sacrament (and it is no magical cure for physical illness, just as it is not a kind of religious alternative to medicine), it should not be supposed that healing has not taken place. For always when the sacrament is administered there is a bestowal of that strengthening of the inward self, which assists the sick person in bearing his or her illness more trustfully and more confidently, and, if it is God's will that he or she should die, to die with a renewed sense of peace and of God's presence and goodness. It is a happy fact that the sacrament of the anointing of the sick is now used more widely throughout the Church, and it is good that many of the misconceptions about it – not least that is is a sacrament solely for the use of the dying – have been replaced by a deeper understanding of its true nature. Here, in the Church's ministry of healing, centred upon the use of the Sacrament of Holy Unction and upon the Laying on of hands with Prayer (the latter being a ministry which may be carried out by any Christian whose calling to it is recognised by the Church), is an area in which there is a real deliverance from evil. For sickness, whilst it may be used by God for some good purpose, cannot be seen as imposed by God as part of his predetermined will. Rather, the Church's ministry of healing is carried out in accordance with the command of Jesus (Matt. 10:8) and is a means by which his grace is bestowed. A further area in which the petition 'deliver us from evil' is put into effect, and one which relates to the ministry of healing carried out by the Church, is the area which is sometimes called the Ministry of Deliverance. This, in extreme cases, may involve the exorcising from people and places of malign spiritual powers and presences which have taken possession and which need to be resisted and removed. This is an area which is both specialized and fairly uncommon, but it is, nonetheless, an area in which deliverance from evil takes place very obviously by the power and grace of the risen Christ.

The source of all grace and power for the deliverance of God's people from evil lies in the saving work of Our Lord Jesus Christ, in that victory over sin and death which was brought about by his dying and rising. All deliverance from evil is made possible by that saving action, and is a laying-hold on the power which flows from it. That dying and rising of Christ is for Christians the new Passover: it was foreshadowed and pictured in the freeing of God's ancient people from slavery in Egypt and their entrance into the promised land. That particular deliverance from evil in former times points foward towards the ultimate deliverance from all evil, moral, natural, and spiritual, which will find its culmination at Christ's future coming in glory, when the dead will be raised and his mighty work of delivering all creation from evil will reach its glorious conclusion.

10

'For the kingdom, the power, and the glory are yours, now and for ever.'

First and foremost in our prayer we should be looking at God. It is inevitable, and indeed natural and right, that we should bring the needs and concerns of ourselves and of other people into our prayer, but those needs must not be dominant. Prayer, as we have seen, is being in God's presence and giving him our attention and our living regard; he, therefore, and he alone must be at the heart and centre of our prayer. The Lord's Prayer, in which Jesus teaches us how to pray, brings this before us very clearly. We begin the prayer by looking at God, recalling that he is our Father in heaven, and asking that his wise and loving rule may be established upon the earth. Only after this do we look at ourselves and at others, asking for the means of life – physical and spiritual – for forgiveness, and for the ability to forgive others. We also ask for strength to resist temptation and for deliverance from evil. And then at the end of the prayer we come back to looking at God himself, rejoicing in the fact that authority, power, and glory are his and will remain his for ever.

It is in the fact of God's authority, power, and glory that Christians find confidence, confidence to face life and to stand rather than fall. They are only too aware of their own weakness. They know themselves to be beset by all kinds of temptation, and they know from past experience what a poor showing they often make in resisting it. Christian know, too, if they are realistic, the strength of evil. They are aware that we are battling 'against cosmic powers, against the authorities and potentates of this dark world, against the superhuman forces of evil in the heavens' (Ephesians 6:12), and that sometimes these things threaten to overwhelm us. The Christian also knows from his or her everyday experience the difficulties and discouragements which have to be faced in following Christ. It is not always easy to practise the disciplines of the Christian life or, for some, to accept the teachings of the Church. For some, being a Christian may mean being taunted and being disadvantaged. For no one, if the Faith is being lived out in a wholehearted way, will the Christian profession be an easy option. Jesus tells all his disciples to take up the Cross and follow him (Luke 9:23), and just as we hope and expect to follow him through death into life, so here on earth we must expect to follow him into difficulty and even into defeat. Following Jesus, participating in the human experience in which he has participated, is fundamental to discipleship. It is often hard, but we find our strength and our confidence in the fact that authority, power, and glory belong to God. They have been wonderfully demonstrated in the resurrection of Jesus from the dead, and this resurrection of Jesus is the sign and the guarantee of our hope. As Christians baptized into Christ and nourished at the altar with his risen and glorified Body and Blood, we are already living the life of Easter and thereby experiencing the power and glory of God. The Christ to whom we belong and who gives himself to us has conquered the powers of darkness, and his victory only awaits its final consummation. Put crudely, we are on the winning side, the side to which ultimate and unending victory is assured. This is the ground of our confidence, the reason why we are not downcast and overwhelmed by the fact that we are sharing in the Cross during the course of our pilgrimage through this world.

The kingdom belongs to God, and as members of the Church we are living as parts of that kingdom. An important part of the life of the Church here on earth, and one which gives particular help, encouragement and indeed joy to Christians, is the pattern of the Church's year, with its procession of seasons, feasts and fasts. In its course we are reminded of the events of salvation, and in a special way it heightens our awareness of living in God's kingdom and of experiencing in our own lives, and in the life of the whole Christian community, the power and the glory of God. The Church's year also gives Christians a framework for their spirituality and a balance within it; a balance between joy and sorrow, penitence and praise, and more particularly a balance between the various part of prayer, thanksgiving, confession, intercession, and adoration. The prayer, the spirituality, of most Christians is influenced, directed, and even formed by the pattern of the Church's year to a greater extent than is perhaps realised. It provides substance and shape not only for the liturgical or public prayer of the Church, but also for our private prayer; a framework of mood and material which comes from the readings, hymns, prayers and ceremonies which are special to the different days and seasons of the Calendar, and which bring divine action before our corporate and individual consciousness.

The yearly cycle begins with the month-long season of Advent which precedes Christmas. The theme of this season is the Coming of Jesus, and as the Church prepares to celebrate his coming in the past at Bethlehem, it also meditates upon how he will come in the future, as Lord and Judge, and upon how he comes in the present, most particularly in his word and in his sacrament. Advent is a solemn season; the coming in judgement is the particular aspect of Christ's coming which is emphasised. This is a solemn theme, and one which necessarily causes Christians to consider their need for repentance and amendment of life. The celebration of the birth of Jesus at Christmas, together with the events which comprise his Epiphany or Showing, make one of the most joyful times in the Church's year. A time when we contemplate the love of God made manifest in the Incarnation, God giving himself to his world and sharing in our common humanity in order to redeem it. The Christmas season ends with our commemoration of the Baptism of Jesus, and not many weeks later the season of Lent begins, when the Church prepares for the celebration of the saving work of Christ in the course of Holy Week and Easter.

Lent is a time for concentrated self-discipline and endeavour, a time when the Christian 'goes into training', and seeks to renew his or her vigour in the practice of the Christian life; a time too when special emphasis is placed upon growth in holiness and consequently upon the repentance and overcoming of sin. Advent and Lent are both thought of as penitential seasons, but the note of penitence is more marked in Lent, with its ancient disciplines of prayer, fasting, and almsgiving. Holy Week, which begins with the commemoration of Christ's entry into Jerusalem on Palm Sunday, and includes the commemoration of the Last Supper on Maundy Thursday and the crucifixion of Jesus on Good Friday, is the focal point of the whole Christian Year, and the ancient and moving liturgies which form its main observances have a unique and treasured place in the spirituality of many Christian people. In the night of Easter Eve and on Easter Day itself the Church celebrates the resurrection of Jesus with great solemnity and joy. This is the high point of the Christian Year, as all Christendom rejoices over Christ's life-giving victory over the grave. This celebration continues throughout the great fifty days of Eastertide, which is the most ancient season of the Christian cycle, having its roots in the Jewish celebration of the entrance into the Promised Land. Eastertide (sometimes called the Great Sunday, from the fact that every Sunday in the year is a celebration of the resurrection, as is every day at Eastertide) ends with the Feast of Pentecost, when Christians celebrate the coming of God the Holy Spirit to the Church. Then the period between Pentecost and the beginning of Advent is 'ordinary time', when, having celebrated the saving actions of Jesus, the Church then meditates upon his teaching and seeks to live out what it professes and proclaims. Towards the end of this period of 'ordinary time' comes the Feast of All Saints, on November 1st, when the grace of God manifested in the saints is celebrated; next day, November 2nd, is the commemoration of All Souls, when we pray for all those who have departed this life. On these two days the Church is reminded of its breadth: that it includes not only those who are battling here on earth, but also the saints who rejoice and reign with Christ in heaven, and those who have died in Christ and now await the fulfilment of his promises when he comes again in glory.

All Souls Day, as it is popularly called, provides a focus for our prayer for the departed, and in rather the same kind of way All Saints Day provides a focus for our veneration of the Saints, whose individual feast days are scattered throughout the whole of the Church's Year. The saints, those elder members of the Church's family who have loved God and loved their fellow human beings in a truly heroic way, play a significant part in the lives of their fellow Christians. In their earthly lives their mirrored Christ, mirrored him with fewer of those distortions of which we are so aware in our own lives. They show us in a thousand different situations and places what it means to be Christ-like, and what constitutes authentic Christian living. They have been more responsive to our common vocation to be other-Christs than we have, and as other-Christs they show us in practical terms what it means to be living as part of the kingdom which is now and for ever. In them we can catch glimpses of the power and the glory of God, for they act not only as mirrors but as windows too. The saints instruct us, but more than that they inspire us. For we see in them the supreme goodness and the wonderful attractiveness of Jesus. The saints help us to realise that death to self in order to come alive to God is nothing less than the way to real and lasting happiness. We are inspired to follow them in following Christ so that we may enter with them into his presence. They challenge us too, because set besides their wholehearted acceptance and living-out of the life of the kingdom we recognise our lukewarmness and the partial character of our love of God and commitment to him. And so Christians pursuing their pilgrimage are mindful of the saints. They see them as one of God's special gifts to the Church, and they know that they need both the challenge and inspiration which the saints provide. But more than this, they know also that they can benefit greatly from the prayers

---

of the saints, and they therefore seek the assistance of these brothers and sisters in heaven just as they seek the prayers of their brothers and sisters here on earth. We are, the Christian knows, 'knit together in one communion and fellowship' within the kingdom of God. The Communion of Saints is something real and vibrant, and is in itself a cause of confidence and joy.

'For the kingdom, the power, and the glory are yours, now and for ever'. The prayer which Jesus taught his disciples ends with this confident assertion, and thereby reminds us that confidence should be a characteristic of every disciple of Our Lord Jesus Christ. A confidence which is founded wholly upon the power, the glory, and the love of God; upon what God has done in creation and redemption, and upon what he is doing now in the hearts and lives of his faithful people. Each year when the Easter Candle is blessed and lit on Easter Eve, the Christian hears the words 'Christ yesterday and today, the beginning and the end, Alpha and Omega; all time belongs to him and all ages; to him be glory and power, through every age and for ever.' These words encapsulate our hope and our belief. They express the deepest conviction of the person who has purposed to be a Christian.

INDEX

133

Index